Priscilla Hauser's
Decorative
Painting Secrets

Priscilla Hauser's
Decorative Painting Secrets

PRISCILLA HAUSER

Sterling Publishing Co., Inc.
New York

Prolific Impressions Production Staff:

Editor: Mickey Baskett
Copy: Phyllis Mueller
Graphics: Lampe Farley Communications, Inc.
Styling: Lenos Key
Photography: Jerry Mucklow, Steve Wilcox Photography
Administration: Jim Baskett

Every effort has been made to insure that the information presented is accurate. Since we have no control over physical conditions, individual skills, or chosen tools and products, the publisher disclaims any liability for injuries, losses, untoward results, or any other damages which may result from the use of the information in this book. Thoroughly read the instructions for all products used to complete the projects in this book, paying particular attention to all cautions and warnings shown for that product to ensure their proper and safe use.

Library of Congress Cataloging-in-Publication Data Available

10 9 8 7 6 5 4 3 2 1
Published by Sterling Publishing Company, Inc.
387 Park Avenue South, New York, N.Y. 10016
Produced by Prolific Impressions, Inc.
160 South Candler St., Decatur, GA 30030
©2001 by Prolific Impressions, Inc.

Distributed in Canada by Sterling Publishing
c/o Canadian Manda Group, One Atlantic Avenue, Suite 105
Toronto, Ontario, Canada M6K 3E7
Distributed in Great Britain and Europe by Chris Lloyd at Orca Book
Services, Stanley House, Fleets Lane, Poole BH15 3AJ, England
Distributed in Australia by Capricorn Link (Australia) Pty. Ltd.
P.O. Box 704, Windsor, NSW 2756 Australia

Printed in China
All rights reserved
Sterling ISBN 0-8069-2757-7

Acknowledgements

The author wishes to thank the following companies for their generous contribution of supplies for the painting of the projects in this book:

For FolkArt® brand paints, varnishes, sealers, and mediums:
Plaid Enterprises, Inc., Norcross, GA, USA
www.plaidonline.com

For brushes:
My favorite flat brushes are Loew-Cornell's Series 7300. I also prefer Loew-Cornell's Series 7000 round brushes, Series 7350 liner brushes, and Series 7500 filbert brushes.
Loew-Cornell, Inc., Teaneck, NJ, USA
www.loew-cornell.com

For the birdhouse:
Plum Creek
700 N. Golden Key, Suite A-5
Gilbert, AZ 85234 USA

For the twig key keeper:
Country Pleasures
10003 CR 6310
West Plains, MO 65775 USA

For the glass platter & ornaments:
B & B Products
8700 N. 107th Ave. #13
Sun City, AZ 85373 USA
www.etchall.com.

For Masterson Sta-Wet Palette:
Masterson Art Products, Inc., Phoenix, AZ, USA
www.mastersonart.com

This book would not have been possible without the help of:
Naomi Meeks, my angel,
Judy Kimball
Joyce Beebe.

About Priscilla Hauser

She has been called "first lady of decorative painting" because of her early involvement in the teaching of the craft and her key role in organizing the first meeting of the National Society of Tole and Decorative Painters on October 22, 1972. Since that first meeting, attended by Priscilla and 21 others, the organization has thrived, and so has Priscilla.

From her beginning efforts as a tole painter in the early 1960s, when she took classes at a YMCA in Raytown, Missouri, Priscilla Hauser has become a world-renowned teacher and author and the decorative painting industry's ambassador to the world. She has traveled to teach in Canada, Japan, Argentina, and The Netherlands and has instructed extensively throughout the United States and at her Studio by the Sea in Panama City Beach, Florida. Besides teaching, Priscilla has illustrated her techniques through books, magazine articles, videos, and television. The results of her teaching program have led to an accreditation program for teachers.

Priscilla says to everyone, "I can teach you to paint. Come paint with me in my beautiful Studio by the Sea! You will learn the basics: brush strokes, double loading, blending, and proper preparation of surfaces. You'll even learn some pen-and-ink techniques and some fabric painting." Priscilla's seminars are extremely valuable to the beginner as well the more advanced painter. Her methods teach the newcomer and strengthen the experienced. The seminars last five-and-a-half days and, after studying for 100 hours, you can become accredited with the Priscilla Hauser Program.

To receive seminar details, send for Priscilla Hauser's Seminar Brochure and Schedule, P.O. Box 521013, Tulsa, OK 75152-1013.

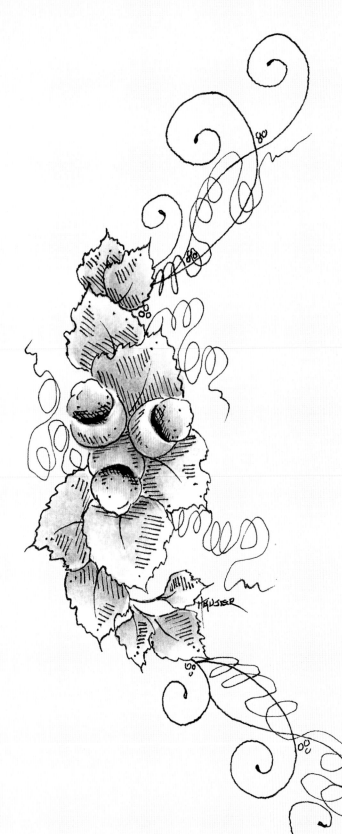

TABLE OF CONTENTS

"Come into my world of painting, and share my secrets for painting beautiful flowers for each month of the year."

Through the many wonderful years I have spent traveling, teaching, and painting, I have kept a diary with notes of where I was, what I saw, and what I did. In creating this diary of flower painting, I have shared some of these adventures with you. Eleven months of the year—January through November—highlight different flowers to paint on a variety of surfaces. For December, I present a dozen flower-themed ornaments painted with washes of color and finished with inked details. I have included numerous worksheets that show you my techniques, step by step.

In every seminar I teach, I quote the words from a song called "Never Never Land," which speaks of dreams and blue skies, a place you can't find on a map, a place that's in your heart. That's where I go when I paint.

Painting fills your mind, I tell my students. After you've learned to concentrate, learned the strokes, and learned how to float, painting becomes a fabulous adventure. You will see things as you've never seen them before.

I hope you'll take the time to learn the basic brush strokes and the basic technique of floating. If you do this, your flower painting won't look basic. It will look warm, beautiful, and wonderful. Please enjoy painting the flowers of the month for yourself, and share them with others. □

Priscilla S. Hauser

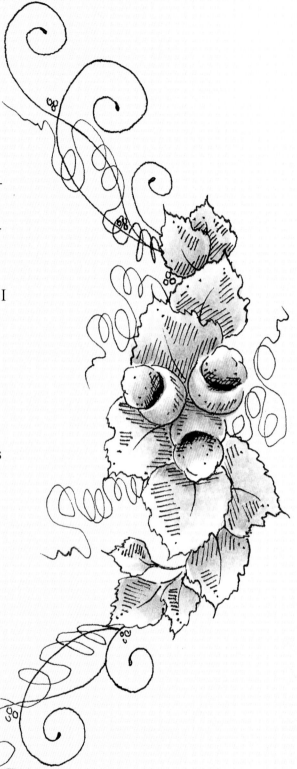

Supplies

Paints

The projects in this book were painted with **artist's acrylic paints**. These rich, creamy, opaque paints come in squeeze bottles and are available at art supply and craft stores. They have true pigment color names, just like oils. Their pigment is brilliant, and you can blend them and move them much in the same way as oil paints by using painting mediums.

Pre-mixed **acrylic craft paints** are available in hundreds of colors. These are not true pigment colors — but blended colors. They have the same consistency as the artist's acrylic paints and can also be used for decorative painting the same way as the artist's acrylic paints. In this book, I use them occasionally to undercoat a design and many times for basecoating. Both these paints are compatible with one another.

Mediums

Mediums are liquids or gels that are mixed with paint for achieving specific effects. They are sold along with the artist's acrylic paints. You will need floating medium and blending gel medium for each and every painting project.

Floating medium is used to thin the paint so that it can be used for floating a color. The brush is filled with the floating medium, a corner of the brush is then filled with color. After the brush is blended on the palette, the color is brushed along the edge of a design element to create a shading or highlighting.

Blending gel medium is used to keep paint wet and moving. The medium is painted onto the surface in the area of the design where it is being painted. The design is painted immediately while the blending medium is still wet.

Glass and tile medium is used to make painting easier on slick surfaces. If you are painting on glass, metal, glazed ceramics, or candles— you will need this medium. It is painted onto the surface of the project, in the area where the design is going to be painted. After it has dried, the design is painted.

Glazing medium is used to thin the paint so that the mixture can be used as antiquing. The glazing medium is mixed with the paint on a palette or in a small container until a very thin transparent consistency is reached. This medium can also be used as a substitute for floating medium. It works in the same way but has a longer blending time.

Photo shows mixing paint and glazing medium on palette to create a wash or an antiquing glaze.

Palette of Colors

These colors were used to paint the projects in this book:

Artist's Acrylic Paints

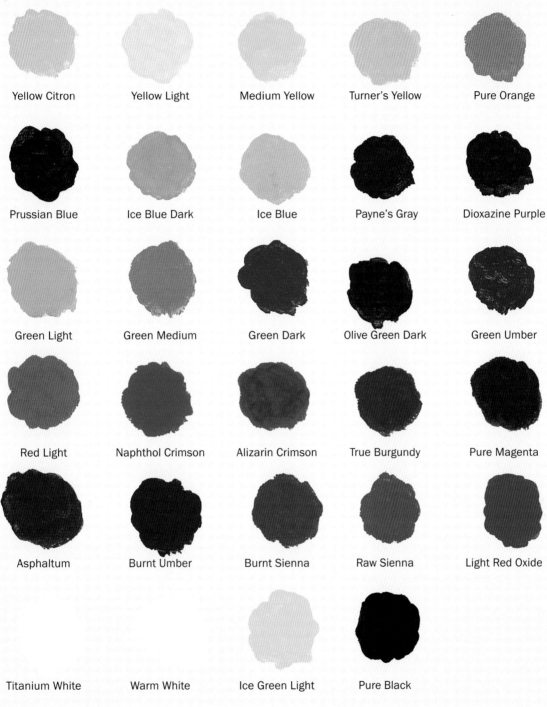

Yellow Citron   Yellow Light   Medium Yellow   Turner's Yellow   Pure Orange

Prussian Blue   Ice Blue Dark   Ice Blue   Payne's Gray   Dioxazine Purple

Green Light   Green Medium   Green Dark   Olive Green Dark   Green Umber

Red Light   Naphthol Crimson   Alizarin Crimson   True Burgundy   Pure Magenta

Asphaltum   Burnt Umber   Burnt Sienna   Raw Sienna   Light Red Oxide

Titanium White   Warm White   Ice Green Light   Pure Black

Acrylic Craft Paints

Clover   Bayberry   Sunflower   Lemonade

Lipstick Red   Periwinkle   Taffy   White

Brushes

THERE ARE MANY DIFFERENT TYPES OF BRUSHES, and different-shaped brushes do different things. You will need the four types of brushes, in various sizes to do your decorative painting. The individual project instructions list the sizes of brushes needed for that particular project.

FLAT BRUSHES
Flat brushes are designed for brush strokes and blending. These brushes do most of the painting of the designs.

ROUND BRUSHES
Round brushes are used primarily for stroking—we seldom blend with them. They can also be used for some detail work.

FILBERT BRUSHES
Filbert brushes are a cross between a flat and a round brush. They are generally used for stroking, but can also be used for blending.

LINER BRUSHES
Liner brushes are very thin round brushes that come to a wonderful point. Good liner brushes are needed for fine line work.

When it comes to brushes, please purchase the very best that money can buy. They are your tools—the things you paint with. Occasionally, a student says, "Priscilla, I don't want to buy a good brush until I know I can paint." I always tell my students they won't be able to paint if they don't begin with a good brush. You get what you pay for.

Brush strokes are the basis of my decorative painting technique. This book includes excellent brush stroke worksheets for practicing. To use them, lay a sheet of acetate or tracing paper over the top of the worksheets, choose a brush approximately the same size as the brush used on the worksheet, and practice hundreds of strokes on top of mine. (If a hundred sounds like a lot, get over it! You will find that painting a hundred strokes happens very quickly.)

Brush types (top to bottom): flat, round, filbert, liner

Brush Care

It's important to clean your brushes properly and keep them in excellent condition. To thoroughly clean them:

1. Gently flip-flop each brush back and forth in water until all the paint is removed, rinsing them thoroughly. Never slam brushes into a container and stir them.
2. Work brush cleaner through the hairs of the brush in a small dish and wipe the brush on a soft, absorbent rag. Continue cleaning until there is no trace of color on the rag.
3. Shape the brush with your fingers and store it so nothing can distort the shape of the hairs. Rinse the brush in water before using again.

Photo 1: Rinse brush in water until paint is removed.

Photo 2: Work brush cleaner through the hairs of the brush in a small container.

Palette

YOU WILL NEED THIS FOR ALL YOUR PAINTING projects. I like to use a wet palette. Some people prefer a wax-coated or dry palette for acrylics; however, I prefer a palette that stays wet since acrylics dry to quickly. Palettes can be found where decorative painting supplies are sold. A wet palette consists of a plastic tray that holds a wet sponge and special paper. To use palette:

1. Soak the sponge in water until saturated. Do not wring out, but place the very wet sponge into tray. (**photo 1**)

2. Soak the paper that comes with the palette in water for 12-24 hours. Place the paper on top of the very wet sponge. (**photo 2**)

3. Wipe the surface of the paper with a soft, absorbent rag to remove the excess water. (**photo 3**)

4. When paints are placed on top of a properly prepared wet palette (**photo 4**), they will stay wet for a long time.

Photo 1. Place the wet sponge in the plastic tray.

Photo 2. Place soaked palette paper on top of the sponge.

Photo 3. Wipe the surface of the paper to remove excess water.

Photo 4. Squeeze paint on palette.

Surfaces

ALMOST ANY SURFACE TYPE CAN BE USED with these type of paints. Wood is the most common surface for decorative painting, yet other surfaces such as glass, metal, papier mache, and even fabric can be decorated.

For the projects in this book, I have painted on a variety of surfaces—wooden architectural fragments, an enameled tin watering can, baskets, a lamp base, a glass plate, and glass ornaments—to name a few. Unfinished wood items, papier mache, plain glass items, and metal surfaces can be found in craft shops and home improvement centers. Other places to look for items to paint are department stores, antique shops, and from mail order catalogs. My designs are versatile and can be adapted to all manner of surfaces. Let your imagination be your guide.

Unfinished Wood Preparation:

1. Sand piece thoroughly with medium, then with fine sandpaper. Wipe with a tack rag.

2. When using acrylic paints for basecoating a piece, it is usually not necessary to seal the wood. However, if there are knotholes or areas where wood is green, I apply a light coat of matte acrylic varnish to seal the flaw before applying paint. In general, however, I don't seal raw wood before painting because paint adheres better to unsealed wood.

3. If the sealer has raised the grain of the wood, sand lightly with fine sandpaper. Wipe with a tack rag.

Different types of wood require different preparations. For example, if you are going to stain the piece, you will not need to seal the piece. Individual project instructions will tell what to do on the types of surfaces shown.

Basecoating:

Basecoating is applying paint to a project surface you wish to decorate before the design is transferred to the surface.

1. With a sponge brush, apply a generous amount of paint. Let dry.

2. Sand with a piece of a brown paper bag with no printing on it to smooth the painted wood.

3. Apply a second coat of the base color, if needed for coverage. Let dry.

4. Use a piece of brown paper bag to smooth the surface again. (Sometimes a third coat of paint is necessary to achieve full coverage.)

Finish:

A finish is needed to protect the painted surface. For wood surfaces, I apply two or more coats of **waterbase varnish** as follows:

1. After the painting is thoroughly dry and cured, using a **synthetic bristle brush or a sponge brush,** apply a coat of brush-on varnish.

2. When the varnish is dry, rub the surface with a piece of a brown paper bag with no printing on it to smooth the surface.

3. Apply a final coat of varnish or a coat of clear **paste wax**.

Other Supplies

THESE ARE THE ADDITIONAL SUPPLIES that are needed for each project. These are not listed in the individual project instructions, however, you will need to gather them for each and all of the projects.

Sandpaper - I use sandpaper for smoothing unfinished or sometimes finished wood surfaces. Sandpaper comes in various grades from very fine to very coarse.

Tack Rag - A tack rag is a piece of cheesecloth or other soft cloth that has been treated with a mixture of varnish and linseed oil. It is very sticky. Use it for wiping a freshly sanded surface to remove all dust particles. When not in use, store the tack rag in a tightly sealed jar.

Brown Paper Bags - I use pieces of brown paper bags with no printing on them to smooth surfaces after basecoating and between coats of varnish.

Tracing Paper - I like to use a very thin, transparent tracing paper for tracing designs. I use a **pencil** for tracing.

Chalk, White and Colored - I use chalk for transferring the traced design to the prepared painting surface. Chalk will easily wipe away and not show through the paint. This is why I prefer it to graphite paper. Do not buy the dustless kind.

Graphite Paper - Occasionally, I use White or gray graphite paper to transfer my design. However, I try to avoid using it because the lines may show through the paint. It can also make smudges on the background that are not easily removed.

Stylus - Use a stylus tool for transferring your traced design to the prepared surface. A pencil or a ballpoint pen that no longer writes also may be used.

Palette Knife - Use a palette knife for mixing and moving paint on your palette or mixing surface. I use a straight-blade palette knife made of flexible steel.

100% Cotton Rags - Use rags for wiping your brushes. *Here's a Tip: Use only 100% cotton rags for wiping your brush. Try the knuckle test: For 15 seconds, rub your knuckles on the rag that you wipe your brush on. If your knuckles bleed, think of what that rag is doing to the hairs of your brush!* You could also use soft, absorbent **paper towels** for wiping brushes.

Water Basin - Use a water basin or other container filled with water for rinsing brushes.

Transferring a Design with Chalk

1. Neatly trace the pattern of the design onto tracing paper. You may use a pencil or a pen. It is not necessary to trace shading lines or curlicues. (**photo 1**)

2. Turn over the traced design. Firmly go over the traced lines on the back with chalk. (**photo 2**) Do not scribble all over the tracing with the chalk.

3. Shake off the excess chalk dust, being careful not to inhale the particles.

4. Position the design on the prepared surface, chalk side down. Using a stylus, go over the lines. (**photo 3**) Don't press so hard that you make indentations in the surface. The chalk will be transferred to your surface. Chalk is easily removed and it dissolves as you paint over it.

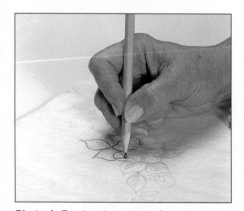
Photo 1. Tracing the pattern from the book.

Photo 2. Going over the lines with chalk on the back of the tracing.

Photo 3. Transferring the pattern lines with a stylus.

Painting Terms

Basecoating • Preparing and painting your project surface before the decorative painting is applied.

Basic Brush Strokes • Basic brush strokes are done with round and flat brushes. Brush strokes are like the letters of the alphabet. They are easy to learn, but they do require practice. Learning these are very important as they are the basis for all of your painting. For example, if you are painting a flower petal, such as a daisy — paint each petal with one brush stroke such as a teardrop. Use as few strokes as possible to paint each part of the design.

Color Wash • A color wash is an application of very thin paint. Actually, one could say it is water with just a little color in it that is applied over a painted surface to add a blush of color. A wash can also be made with glazing medium and a bit of color.

Consistency • Consistency describes the thickness or thinness of the paint. You need different consistencies for different techniques. When you do brush strokes, the paint must be a creamy consistency. When you do linework, the paint must be very thin like the consistency of ink. If paint is too thick, add a few drops of water to the paint puddle on your palette and mix with a palette knife until proper consistency is reached.

Contrast • Contrast is the sharp difference between two or more colors. When two colors meet, one edge must be light (usually the top edge) and the other edge or shadowed area must be dark. Contrast gives life to your painting.

Curing • When something is dry to the touch, it is not cured. If something is cured, it is dry all the way through. I often explain curing with this analogy: If you fall down and skin your knee and it bleeds, it's wet. When the scab forms, it's dry. When the new skin grows, it's cured.

I am frequently asked how long it takes a painted piece to cure. There is no right answer — curing depends upon the temperature, air circulation, humidity, the paint color used, and the thinness or thickness of the paint. When a piece is cured, it feels warm and dry to the touch. Curing can take three hours or several weeks.

Double-Loading • Double-loading is a technique of loading the brush with two colors of paint. Using two different puddles of paint, load half of the brush with the lighter color and the other half with the darker color. Blend by stroking your brush many, many times on the palette on one side of the brush, then turn the brush over and stroke on the other side. It takes many strokes to prime a brush and get it good and full of paint.

Outlining • Most of the time, I outline with a #1 liner brush. (It's possible to outline with the very fine point of any good brush.) When outlining, the brush should be full of paint that has been thinned to the consistency of ink.

Undercoating • Undercoating is neatly and smoothly painting a design or part of a design solidly on the basecoated project surface. Your strokes, shading, and highlighting will be done on top of this undercoated design.

Wash • See "Color Wash."

Painting Tips

• When loading brush with a different color, but one that is in the same color family, it is preferable to wipe brush on a damp paper towel to remove excess paint before loading into a new color. Avoid rinsing brush too often in water.

• When loading your brush with a color in a different color family, the brush does not need to be thoroughly cleaned. Simply rinse in water and blot brush on a paper towel to remove excess water. Then load brush with a new color.

• Sometimes I paint with a "dirty brush."

Leaving some of the color in the brush from another element seems to blend the colors together better. For example, if I want to add a reddish tint to a leaf, I will leave a little green in my brush when I load the red so that the colors can "marry" together.

Skills

Using a Round Brush

Round brushes are used primarily for stroking—we seldom blend with them. They come in a variety of sizes. Practice your round brush strokes on the Brush Stroke Worksheets.

Loading the Brush

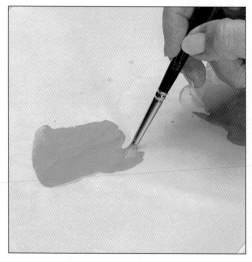

Photo 1. Squeeze paint onto your palette. If needed thin your paint with a thinning medium such as glazing medium or water. Paint should be a creamy consistency.

Photo 2. Load brush by picking up paint from edge of puddle.

Brush Stroke Tips

- For brush strokes, the paint should have a thin, flowing consistency.

- Be sure your brush is full with paint so you don't run out of paint mid-stroke.

- While I don't deliberately get paint up in the ferrule, I don't worry about it. If you clean your brush properly, you will have no problems.

- Always use a fine brush in excellent condition. Choose brushes from a quality manufacturer that stands behind its products.

- Make a flag with a piece of tape on the handle of the paintbrush. When painting strokes, with the exception of the half-circle, the flag should not wave, and you should not twist the brush in your fingers. You simply touch, press, pull, and lift. When you paint the u-stroke, the brush is pivoting in your fingers.

Teardrop or Polliwog Stroke

Photo 1. Touch on the tip of the brush and apply pressure.

Photo 2. Gradually lift and drag straight down. Turning the brush slightly left or right forces the hairs back together to form a point.

1.

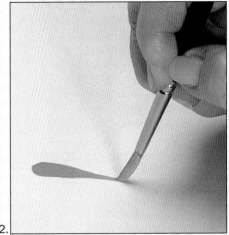

2.

Comma Stroke - Left

Photo 1. Angle the tip of the brush toward the corner of the practice page. Touch and apply pressure.

Photo 2. Begin lifting and pulling to the inside edge of the brush, dragging until a point is formed.

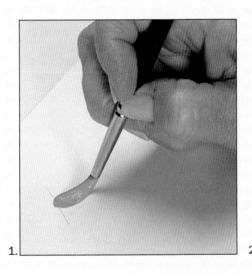

1.

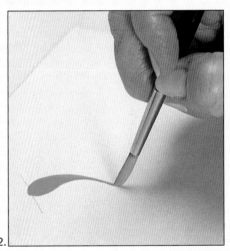

2.

Comma Stroke - Right

This stroke is done in the same way as the left comma stroke, but the tip of the brush is angled to the right corner.

1.

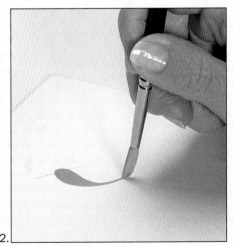

2.

Using a Filbert Brush

The filbert is a variation of the round brush and it is used in much the same way. Notice that the stoke is slightly different looking with a filbert brush.

Comma Stroke - Left

Photo 1. Angle the tip of the brush toward the left corner.
Touch and apply pressure.

Photo 2. Begin to pull and lift, leaning to the inside edge of the brush. Drag to a point.

1.

2.

Comma Stroke - Right

Photo 1. Angle the tip of the brush to the right corner. Touch and apply pressure.

Photo 2. Pull the brush. Begin lifting and pulling to the inside edge of the brush, dragging it until a point is formed.

1.

2.

Using a Flat Brush

Flat brushes are designed for brush strokes and blending. They come in many different sizes. Flat brush strokes or any type of stroke may be painted in a single color. These photos show the brush being double-loaded. The procedure is the same if you are using a single color. Practice your flat brush strokes on the Brush Stroke Worksheets that follow.

Double-Loading

Double-loading involves loading your brush with two colors. Be sure to thin paint with water to a flowing consistency and push it with a palette knife to form a neat puddle with a clean edge.

Photo 1. Stroke up against the edge of the light color 30 times, so half of the brush is loaded with paint and the other half is clean.

Photo 2. Turn the brush over and stroke up against the edge of the dark color 20 times.

Photo 3. Blend, blend, blend one side of the brush on your palette.

Photo 4. Turn the brush over and blend, blend, blend on the other side, keeping the dark color in the center.

Photo 5. Go back and pick up more light paint on the brush.

Photo 6. Go back to the blending spot on your palette and blend some more.

Photo 7. Go back and pick up some more dark color.

Photo 8. Go back to the blending spot on your palette and blend some more. Continue doing this until your brush is full.

Photo 9. Here is a correctly double-loaded brush. You don't want a space between the two colors; you want them to blend into each other.

Line Stroke

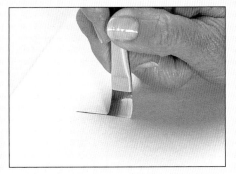

Photo 1. Stand the brush on its flat or chisel edge, perpendicular to the orientation of the basic flat stroke. The handle should point straight up. Pull the brush toward you. Don't press the brush down, as this will thicken and distort the line.

Basic Stroke

Photo 1. Touch the length of the flat or chisel edge of the brush to your surface.

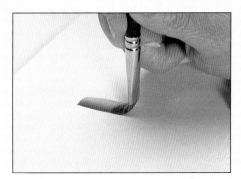

Photo 2. Press the brush down and pull it toward yourself, holding the pressure steady. Lift the brush smoothly at the end of the stroke.

Comma Stroke - Angled Left

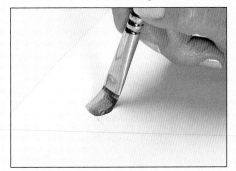

Photo 1. Touch the length of the flat (chisel) edge of the brush at an angle to the right corner of the practice page. *Tip: Drawing the roof of a house with a pencil when you practice may help you find the correct angle.*

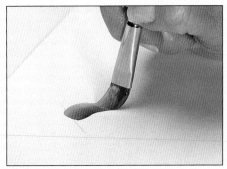

Photo 2. Press down and pull the brush, then lift the brush gradually back up to its flat edge as you pull it to the left. Don't pick up the brush too quickly, or hold the pressure too long.

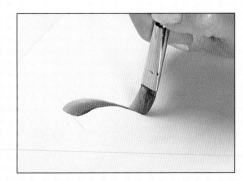

Photo 3. Drag to a point.

Comma Stroke - Angled Right

Photo 1. Touch the length of the flat (chisel) edge of the brush at an angle to the right corner of the practice page. *Tip: Drawing the roof of a house in pencil when you practice may help you find the correct angle.*

Photo 2. Press down and pull the brush, then lift the brush gradually back up to its flat edge as you pull it to the right. Don't pick up the brush too quickly, or hold the pressure too long.

Photo 3. Drag to a point.

S-Stroke Left

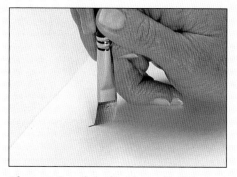

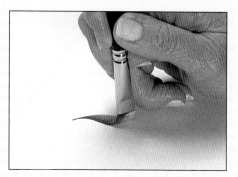

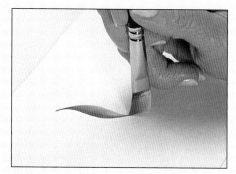

Photo 1. Stand the brush on the flat or chisel edge, angled to the left corner of your practice sheet, with the handle pointing straight up.

Photo 2. Pull, letting the brush roll to the left. Gradually apply pressure.

Photo 3. Pull, lifting slowly back up to the flat (chisel) edge at the end of the stroke.

S-Stroke - Right

Reverse the angle and direction for a right S-stroke. *Tip: Use a pencil to draw S-strokes as a guide. Do your strokes over the pencil marks while practicing, keeping the pencil line in the middle of your brush stroke.*

U-Stroke

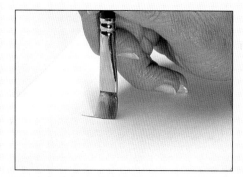

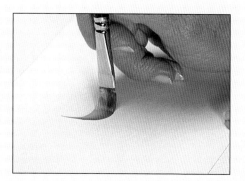

Photo 1. Touch the brush on the flat or chisel edge with the handle pointing straight up.

Photo 2. Pull the brush toward you, gradually applying pressure.

Photo 3. Lift the brush away from you just as gradually, back to the flat edge. This stroke can be reversed for an upside-down U-stroke.

Half-Circle Stroke

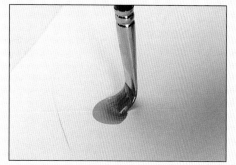

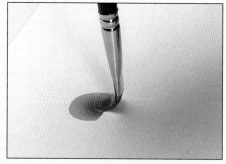

Photo 1. Touch the brush on the flat or chisel edge. Press the brush down.

Photo 2. Holding the pressure steady, pivot or roll the brush so that you create a half circle.

Photo 3. Lift. Note: This is the only time the flag on your brush should wave, as you deliberately pivot the brush in this stroke.

Using a Liner Brush

Liner brushes are the long, thinner members of the round brush family. The bristles come to a wonderful point. Liner brushes are used for fine line work. Practice your liner brush strokes on the Brush Stroke Worksheets.

Loading the Brush

Photo 1. Thin paint with water until it is the consistency of ink.

Photo 2. Fill the brush full of paint by pulling it through paint edge. Twist brush as you pull it out of puddle. this will form a nice pointed tip. When you are using the brush hold it straight up.

Teardrop Stroke

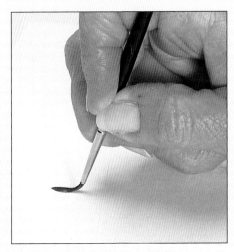

Photo 1. Fill brush with paint of a thin consistency; touch, apply pressure.

Photo 2. Begin pulling and lifting.

Photo 3. Drag to a point.

Comma Stroke - Angled Left

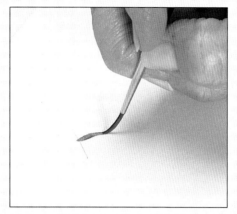

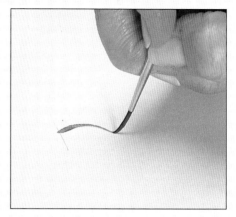

Photo 1. Angle the corner of the brush to the left-hand corner of the practice sheet. Touch and apply pressure.

Photo 2. Begin to pull and lift, leaning to the inside edge of the brush.

Photo 3. Drag to a point.

Comma Stroke - Angled Right

1. Angle the corner of the brush to the right-hand corner of the practice sheet; touch, apply pressure.

2. Begin to pull and lift, leaning to the inside edge of the brush.
3. Drag to a point

Curlicues & Squiggles

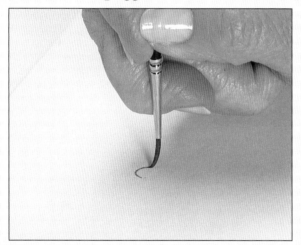

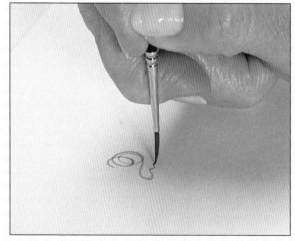

Photo 1. Stand the brush on its point with the handle pointing straight up toward the ceiling.

Photo 2. Slowly move the brush to paint loopy Ms and Ws. Practice several times on your page, Make as many variations as you wish.

Round Brush Strokes

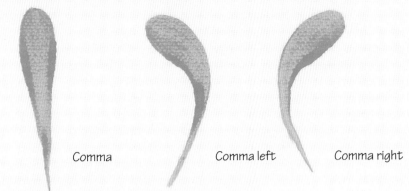

Comma   Comma left   Comma right

Filbert Brush Strokes

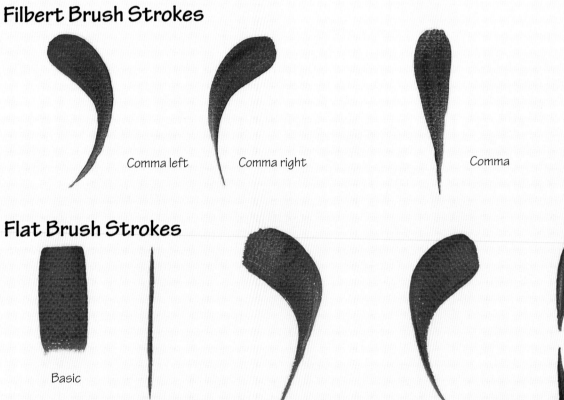

Comma left   Comma right   Comma

Flat Brush Strokes

Basic   Line   Comma left   Comma right   U-Strokes

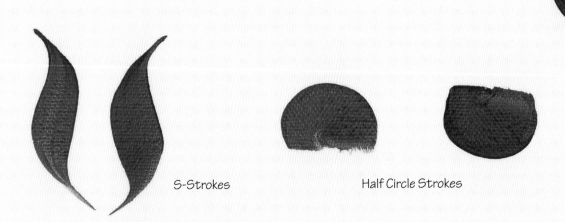

S-Strokes   Half Circle Strokes

Double-Loaded Brush Strokes (using a #12 flat brush)

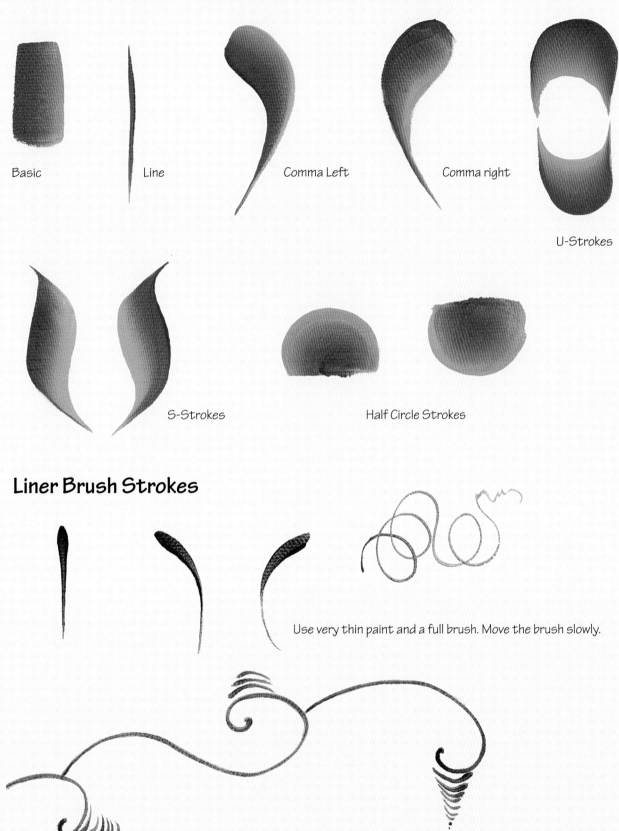

Basic

Line

Comma Left

Comma right

U-Strokes

S-Strokes

Half Circle Strokes

Liner Brush Strokes

Use very thin paint and a full brush. Move the brush slowly.

Floating Technique

Floating is flowing color on a surface. This technique is used for adding the shading and high-lighting to design elements. Before floating, undercoat the area. Let dry. Add a second or even a third coat, if necessary. Let dry. Our example will show the shading and highlighting being floated onto a leaf that has been undercoated in a Bayberry color.

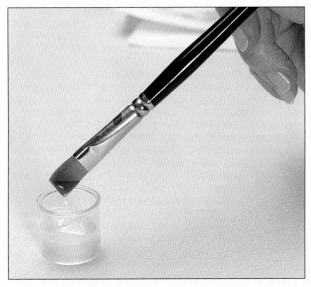

Option A - Floating Medium
Photo 1. Fill as large a brush as possibly you can use on the surface with floating medium.
Option B - Glazing Medium
Use same technique as above. Glazing medium stays wet a little longer.

Option C - Water:
Photo 2. Instead of floating medium, water can be used. Fill as large a brush as possibly you can use on the surface with water and gently pull the brush along the edge of your water basin.

Photo 3. Fill one side of the brush with the shading color by stroking up against the edge of a puddle of paint.

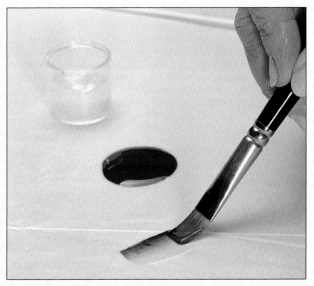

Photo 4. On a matte surface, such as tracing paper or wet palette paper, blend, blend, blend on one side of the brush.

Floating

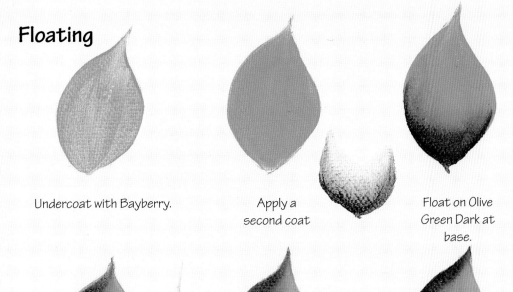

Undercoat with Bayberry.

Apply a second coat

Float on Olive Green Dark at base.

Float on Olive Green Dark on dark side.

Float on a wash of Yellow Light for additional color.

Float on an Ice Blue highlight.

Float on a little Burnt Sienna for additional color.

Add vein with Olive Green Dark, using a liner brush.

Simple Blending

Undercoat with two coats Green Medium.

Float on Green Dark at the base.

Float Green Dark on the dark side. Let dry. Apply blending gel medium.

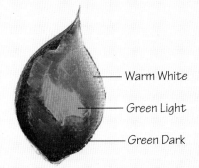

— Warm White

— Green Light

— Green Dark

Add vein with Green Dark, using a liner brush.

Apply colors.

Lightly blend.

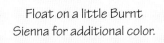

January

January 10, 1983

This morning I went for a walk in the snow. It was gorgeous - with the big flakes slowly floating to the ground. I happen to spot a touch of color in the snow and walked over to investigate. To my delight - a group of yellow and purple crocuses had pushed up through the heavy white blanket. They filled winter with color.

Crocus

Supplies

Artist's Acrylic Paints:
Dioxazine Purple
Green Medium
Green Light
Green Dark
Medium Yellow
Olive Green Dark
Payne's Gray
Pure Magenta
Pure Orange
Raw Sienna
Titanium White

Acrylic Craft Paints:
Periwinkle
Sunflower

Medium:
Floating medium

Brushes:
Flats - #2, #4, #6, #8, #10
Liner - #1

Surface:
Architectural fragment

Additional Supplies:
Gather the additional supplies
that are listed in general
"Supplies" section.

Crocus

Preparation

I wanted to paint this wonderful old fragment just as it was.

1. Clean the fragment using a rag dampened with soap and water. Let dry.
2. Sand lightly to remove any loose paint. Wipe with a tack rag.
3. Neatly trace and transfer the design. (I used colored chalk for transferring.)

Painting

See the Crocus Worksheets on pages 36, 37.

The Leaves:

1. Undercoat the leaves that are closest to the back of the design with Green Dark.
2. Undercoat the leaves in the middle of the design with Green Medium.
3. Undercoat the leaves in the front of the design with Green Light.
4. Using as large a brush as you comfortably can, shade the dark leaves with a float of Olive Green Dark.
5. Shade the medium leaves with a float of Green Dark.
6. Shade the light leaves with a float of Green Dark. Use floating medium or water for the float technique.
7. Mix two parts Green Light and one part Titanium White (2:1). Highlight all of the leaves with this mixture.
8. Float additional shading on the leaves at the ground area with Green Dark. If darker shading is desired, float with a little Olive Green Dark.
9. Paint the little grass-like leaves at the very front with a mixture of Green Light and Titanium White (2:1). Fill a #1 liner brush with this thin mixture and paint the blades of grass.

The Purple Crocus:

Since the purple crocuses are behind the yellow ones, they should be carefully painted first.

1. Neatly undercoat with Periwinkle.
2. Create the dark shadows by floating on Dioxazine Purple. If darker shading is desired, apply a second and even a third float of Dioxazine Purple.
3. To highlight, mix one part Dioxazine Purple and two parts Titanium White (1:2). Float the highlights.
4. Create the linework using a liner brush full of thinned Dioxazine Purple.

The Yellow Crocus:

1. Undercoat the yellow crocus with Sunflower. Let dry.
2. Apply a thin wash of Medium Yellow. Let dry. Apply a second wash of Medium Yellow. Let dry.
3. To shade, apply a float of Raw Sienna in the shaded areas, as shown on the worksheet. Let dry.
4. To deepen the shading, apply a float of Pure Orange over the Raw Sienna shadows. Be careful—not too much! (It will create a beautiful touch.)
5. Mix equal amounts of Pure Orange and Raw Sienna (1:1). Fill a #1 liner with this thinned mixture. Paint the fine lines on the front petal, as shown on the worksheet.
6. Highlight the top of the petals by floating on a mixture of Medium Yellow and Titanium White (1:2). Study this on the worksheet. Let dry and cure.

Finishing

1. Varnish with two or more coats of waterbase varnish. Let dry.
2. Rub with a piece of brown paper bag with no printing on it to smooth the raised surface.
3. Apply a final coat of varnish or rub with paste wax. □

Pattern for January Crocus
Actual Size

Crocus Worksheet

Step 1

Undercoat dark leaves with Green Dark. Shade with Olive Green Dark.

Undercoat medium leaves with Green Medium. Shade with Green Dark.

Undercoat light leaves with Green Light. Shade with Green Dark.

Step 2

Undercoat purple flowers with Periwinkle.

Undercoat yellow flowers with Sunflower.

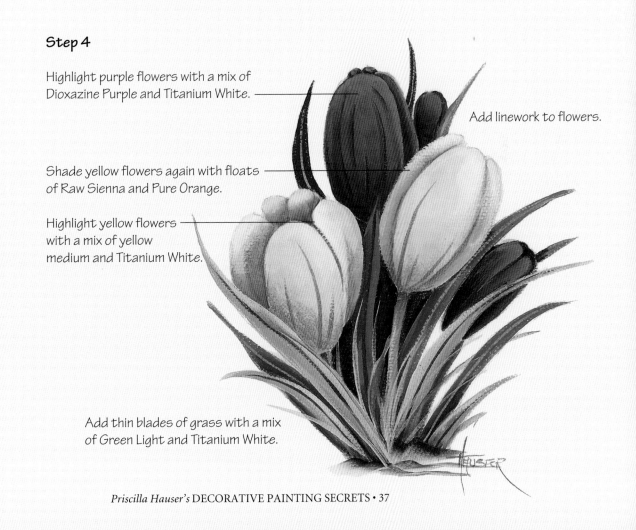

Step 3

Shade purple flowers with floats of Dioxazine Purple.

Shade yellow flowers with floats of Raw Sienna.

Step 4

Highlight purple flowers with a mix of Dioxazine Purple and Titanium White.

Add linework to flowers.

Shade yellow flowers again with floats of Raw Sienna and Pure Orange.

Highlight yellow flowers with a mix of yellow medium and Titanium White.

Add thin blades of grass with a mix of Green Light and Titanium White.

February

February 28, 1974

Driving from Tulsa to my studio in Florida in the early spring, is an incredible experience. It's a rainbow of color with the blooming azaleas and the wild dogwood scattered through the forest. It appears like an impressionistic painting with dots of pink and white floating through the trees.

These beautiful flowers hold special meaning since the legend says that their petals form the cross that our Lord died upon.

Dogwood

Supplies

Artist's Acrylic Paints:
Burnt Umber
Green Light
Olive Green Dark
Payne's Gray
True Burgundy

Acrylic Craft Paints:
Bayberry
White

Mediums:
Floating medium

Brushes:
Flats - #4, #6, #8, #10, #12
Liner - #10/0, #1
Filbert - #4

Surface:
Architectural fragment

Additional Supplies:
Gather the additional supplies that are listed in general "Supplies" section.

Dogwood

Preparation

I love the old, worn look of this piece.

1. If the paint is flaking off, sand it until no more paint comes off. Wipe with a tack rag. If touch-up is needed, proceed as required.
2. Neatly trace and transfer the design using colored chalk or a well-used piece of gray graphite paper.

Painting

See the Dogwood Worksheet.

The Leaves and Stems:

1. Undercoat the leaves with two coats of Bayberry. Let dry.
2. Paint the stems with two coats of Bayberry, using the liner brush. Let dry.
3. Shade the stems where they come out from behind one another and on the left side with a float of Olive Green Dark.
4. Outline the left side of the stems using the #1 liner and thinned Burnt Umber.
5. Shade at the base of each leaf with a float of Olive Green Dark. Let dry.
6. Shade the tips of a few leaves with a float of Olive Green Dark. Let dry.
7. Shade the left sides of some of the leaves with a float of Olive Green Dark. Let dry.
8. If desired, float True Burgundy on the tips and at the bases of a few leaves. Let dry.
9. Highlight the right sides of the stems using the #1 liner and thinned Green Light. Let dry.

The Dogwood Flowers:

1. Paint each petal with two coats of White, using the #4 filbert brush. Let dry.
2. Shade any flower that comes from under another flower with a float of Payne's Gray.
3. Dab in the centers with Olive Green Dark. Let dry.
4. Using a stylus, add dots of thinned Green Light to the centers. Study the worksheet.
5. Shade the base of each petal with a float of Olive Green Dark. Let dry.
6. Using a liner brush with thinned White, outline each petal. Pull three or four curved lines, following the shape of the petal, from the center out. Let dry.
7. Highlight the tips of the petals with a float of White. Let dry.
8. Paint the v-shape at the end of each petal using a #4 flat brush with a float of True Burgundy. Let dry. Soften with a wash of White. Let dry.
9. Paint the buds in the same manner as the single petal.

Background Shading & Highlights:

1. Shade the background with a float of Burnt Umber. Start next to the flower centers and fade out from there in each direction.
2. Shade at each corner with a float of Burnt Umber. Let dry.
3. Using a liner brush with thinned Green Light, paint a few grass-like lines near the stems and leaves, if desired. Let dry and cure.

Finishing

1. Varnish with two or more coats of waterbase varnish. Let dry.
2. Rub with a piece of brown paper bag with no printing on it to smooth the raised surface.
3. Apply a final coat of varnish or rub with clear paste wax. ☐

Dogwood
Actual Size Pattern

Dogwood Worksheet

Stems & Leaves:

Step 1
Undercoat with two coats of Bayberry.

Step 2
Shade stems and leaves with floats of Olive Green Dark. Outline left side of stems with Burnt Umber.

Step 3
Float True Burgundy at the tips of some leaves.

Flowers

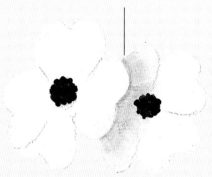

Step 2
Shadow flowers underneath with floats of Payne's Gray.

Dab centers with Olive Green Dark.

Step 1
Undercoat with two coats of White.

Step 3
Shade petals with floats of Olive Green Dark.

Mix Green Light and White and add dots on centers.

Step 4

Outline petals and add curved lines with White.

Float White across the ends of petals.

Step 5

Accent tips of petals with floats of True Burgundy. Let dry.

Apply a wash of White.

March

March 11, 1998

I can smell them as I'm approaching my father's home. The beautiful little Lilies of the Valley — my grandmother's favorite flower and Dad's favorite as well. I'll pick a bouquet of them and paint them on something special for him - - -

Lily of the Valley

Supplies

Artist's Acrylic Paints:
Burnt Umber
Green Light
Ice Blue
Ice Blue Dark
Ice Green Light
Olive Green Dark
Titanium White

Acrylic Craft Paint:
Bayberry

Mediums:
Floating medium
Blending gel medium

Brushes:
Flats - #8, #10, #12
Liners - #1, #10/0
Filberts - #4, #6

Surface
Wooden lamp base with off-White distressed finish

Additional Supplies:
Gather the additional supplies that are listed in general "Supplies" section.

Lily of the Valley

Preparation

This lamp came with a sanded off-white finish. Generally, pieces prepared in this manner are waxed instead of varnished.

1. Sand the lamp with fine sandpaper to remove the wax. Wipe with a cloth.
2. Trace and transfer the leaf design using gray graphite paper.

Painting

See the Lily of the Valley Worksheets on pages 52 and 53.

The Leaves:

1. Undercoat the leaves with two coats of Bayberry. Let dry.
2. Using a #10 or #12 flat brush, shade the leaves with a float of Olive Green Dark at the base of the leaves, under the turns, and at the tip. Let dry.
3. Float Olive Green Dark up the left side of the leaf and up the right side of the center. Let dry. Float with Olive Green Dark again, if needed, to deepen the color.
4. Highlight the right sides of the leaves, the left sides of the center veins, and the tops of the turns with a float of Green Light.
5. Shade the bases of the leaves and the turns with a float of Burnt Umber. Let dry.
6. Highlight the right sides of the leaves and the tops of the turns with a float of Ice Green Light. Let dry.

The Stems:

1. Paint the stems using the liner brush with thinned Green Light.
2. Shade the stems with a float of Olive Green Dark.
3. Highlight with a mixture of equal amounts (1:1) Green Light and Ice Green Light. Let dry.

The Flowers:

1. Transfer the flower design on top of the leaves, using white transfer paper.
2. Paint the oval shape of the flower, using a #4 or #6 filbert with two coats Ice Green Light. Let dry.
3. Shade the left sides of the flowers and the bottoms with a float of Olive Green Dark.
4. Highlight the right sides of the flowers with a float of Titanium White.
5. Using a #10/0 liner brush with thinned Titanium White, paint a line down the right side, the ruffle at the bottom, and the little turned-up sides.
6. Paint the left sides of the turned-up sides with linework of Olive Green Dark. Wash Olive Green Dark inside the bottoms.
7. Accent only above the ruffles with a float of Ice Blue Dark.
8. Tint the flowers on the upper left with a float of Green Light.
9. Highlight down the right sides and across the fronts just above the ruffles with a float of Titanium White.

The Buds:

1. Paint the buds with two coats Ice Green Light. Let dry.
2. Shade the left sides with a float of Olive Green Dark.
3. Highlight the right sides of the buds with a float of Titanium White.
4. Tint upper left portions with a float of Green Light. Let dry.
5. Paint the right sides with either a float of Titanium White or a float of Green Light.

The Shadow:

1. Paint using a #10 flat brush with a wash of Burnt Umber. Let dry.
2. Rub gently with a damp cloth to soften. Let dry and cure.

Finishing

1. Paint the linework in the corners using a #10/0 liner brush with very thin Burnt Umber.
2. If the design appears to be too dark, rub it gently with a damp cloth and let dry or sand gently to fade and wipe away dust.
3. Apply one coat of waterbase varnish or wax with clear paste wax. ☐

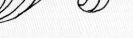

Lily of the Valley
Actual Size Pattern

Lily of the Valley Worksheet

Leaves:

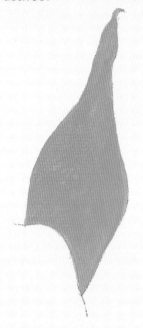

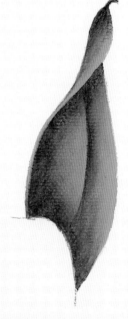

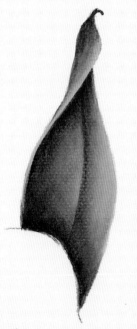

Step 1
Undercoat with two coats of Bayberry. Let dry.

Step 2
Shade with floats of Olive Green Dark. Let dry. Repeat to reinforce.

Step 3
Add highlights with floats of Green Light.

Step 4
Shadow the base and under the turn with Burnt Umber.

Highlight right side and top of turn with Ice Green Light.

Stems:

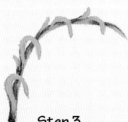

Step 1
Paint with Green Light.

Step 2
Highlight with a mixture of Green Light and Ice Green Light (1:1).

Step 3
Shade with a float of Olive Green Dark.

Lily of the Valley Worksheet

Flowers:

Step 1
Undercoat with two coats of Bayberry.

Step 2
Highlight right sides with Titanium White.

Step 3
Shade left sides and bases with floats of Olive Green Dark.

Step 4
Paint ruffles and right sides with Titanium White. Paint left sides and inside bottoms with Olive Green Dark.

Step 5
Accent with floats of Green Light and Ice Blue Dark.

Step 6
Float Titanium White down the right sides and across the fronts. Let dry.

Apply a wash of Titanium White.

Buds:

Step 1
Undercoat with two coats of Bayberry.

Step 2
Lighten with Titanium White.

Step 3
Shade with Olive Green Dark.

Step 4
Accent with Green Light. Highlight with Titanium White.

Trim:

Step 1
Paint linework with Burnt Umber.

Step 2
Fade the design by sanding or rubbing with a damp cloth.

April

April 2, 1998

Thank goodness it's April. Winter is finally over and spring is blooming everywhere. There are so many types of blossoms. Some so fragrant they make the yard smell wonderful. Blossoms always represent a new beginning. Therefore, I think it's appropriate to paint them on this little white birdhouse which is in the shape of a church. It reminds me so much of the chapel at Carillon Beach, Florida where both our son, Erech, and daughter, Leslie, were married.

Blossoms

Supplies

Artist's Acrylic Paints:
Asphaltum
Burnt Sienna
Burnt Umber
Ice Blue
Olive Green Dark
Titanium White
Yellow Citron
Yellow Light

Acrylic Craft Paint:
Bayberry

Mediums:
Blending gel medium
Glazing medium

Brushes:
Flats - #2, #4, #6, #8, #14
Liner - #1

Surface:
Wooden bird house

Additional Supplies:
Gather the additional supplies that are listed in general "Supplies" section.

Blossoms

Preparation

1. Lightly sand the birdhouse. Wipe with a tack rag.
2. Neatly trace and transfer the design. (I used a piece of well-used gray graphite paper so that the transfer wouldn't be too dark.)

Painting

See the Blossoms Worksheets on pages 60 and 61.

Background Color:

You may apply a background color before or after you do the painting, or you may choose to eliminate it. Do whatever you think will look better—I love the addition of a little background color. Apply the background color using as large a flat brush as you can handle.

1. Mix equal amounts (1:1) Burnt Umber and Asphaltum.
2. Double-load the brush with glazing medium on one side and the paint mixture on the other side. Blend on the palette to soften the color so that the color flows beautifully through the brush from dark to medium to the clear glazing medium.
3. Neatly and carefully pat this color around the outside edge of the design, as shown in the finished photograph and on the worksheet.

The Leaves:

1. Undercoat the leaves with two or more coats Bayberry. Let dry.
2. Using as large a flat brush as you comfortably can, float Olive Green Dark at the bases of the leaves and in the other dark areas, as shown on the worksheet. Use glazing medium for the float. Let dry.

3. Double-load the brush with glazing medium and Ice Blue. Float Ice Blue highlights on the light or right sides of each leaf. Let dry.
4. Paint the stems with Bayberry. Shade with Olive Green Dark. Highlight with Ice Blue.

The Blossoms:

1. Undercoat the petals with two or more coats Titanium White. Let dry.
2. Using as large a flat brush as you comfortably can, float Olive Green Dark at the base of each petal where it touches the center. Let dry. If more color is desired, float Olive Green Dark a second time.
3. Use the #1 liner brush full of thinned Titanium White to neatly outline the petals.

The Centers:

1. Using a tiny flat brush, paint the centers with Yellow Light.
2. To shade, float with Burnt Sienna.
3. Place a dot of Yellow Citron in the center of each one.

4. Using the #1 liner with very thin Burnt Umber, paint hair-like fine lines that flow gracefully from the center onto the petals. Let dry.
5. Apply tiny dots of Olive Green Dark and Titanium White around the centers and out onto the petals, as shown on the worksheet.

The Buds:

1. Paint the buds with Titanium White.
2. Shade by floating on a tiny touch of Olive Green Dark.

The Curlicues:

Paint the curlicues, using a #1 liner full of very thin Burnt Umber. Let dry and cure.

Finishing

1. Varnish with two or more coats waterbase varnish. Let dry.
2. Rub with a piece of brown paper bag with no printing on it to smooth the raised surface.
3. Apply a final coat of varnish or rub with clear paste wax. □

Tips for Painting Curlicues:

- Often, people's reading glasses aren't painting glasses. If you are farsighted, you may need tremendous magnification to paint curlicues. Most people don't realize that they can't see what they are doing.
- To paint beautiful curlicues, use a #1 liner in excellent condition that's full of very thin paint.
- Be sure to hold the handle of the brush so that it points straight up towards the ceiling.
- Paint curlicues slowly, not fast.

Blossoms
Actual Size Pattern

Blossoms Worksheet

Step 1

Undercoat the leaves with several coats Bayberry.

Undercoat petals with Titanium White.

Undercoat centers with Yellow Light.

Step 2

Shade leaves and flower petals with floats of Olive Green Dark.

Shade the centers with floats of Burnt Sienna.

Blossoms Worksheet

Step 3

Add a dot of Yellow Citron or Green Medium to flower centers.

Paint fine linework on the flower petals with thinned Burnt Umber.

Highlight leaves with floats of Ice Blue.

Step 4

Add dots around centers with thinned Olive Green Dark and thinned Titanium White.

Add background color with a mix of Burnt Umber, Asphaltum, and glazing medium.

May

May 18, 1974

What a find! A beautiful old carved piece of what was probably a headboard - in the trash! Well - ofcourse I grabbed it and I'll paint Wisteria on it and it will be a stunning headboard in Kimberly's room. How could anyone throw such a wonderful piece away?

Wisteria

Supplies

Artist's Acrylic Paints:
Burnt Umber
Green Dark
Green Medium
Prussian Blue
Pure Black
Pure Magenta
Raw Sienna
Warm White
Yellow Citron
Yellow Light

Mediums:
Floating medium
Blending gel medium

Brushes:
Flats - #2, #4, #6, #8, #10, #12, #14, #16
Liner - #1
Filbert - #6

Surface:
Architectural fragment (probably from a
bed or dresser)

Additional Supplies:
Gather the additional supplies that are
listed in general "Supplies" section.

Wisteria

Preparation

1. If the paint is flaking, sand the surface to smooth. Wipe with a tack rag.
2. Neatly trace and transfer the design using colored chalk or a well-used piece of gray graphite paper.

Painting

See the Wisteria Worksheets on pages 68 and 69.

The Branches:

1. Mix equal amounts (1:1) Raw Sienna and Burnt Umber. Undercoat with this mixture.
2. Using as large a brush as you comfortably can, float (using floating medium) Burnt Umber in all shadowed areas, as shown on the worksheet.

The Leaves:

1. Undercoat the leaves with two or more coats Green Medium. Let dry.
2. Using as large a flat brush as you comfortably can, float Green Dark at the base of each leaf. Let dry.

The Wisteria Bud:

1. Apply blending gel medium.
2. Apply Pure Magenta, Prussian Blue, and Yellow Citron, as shown on the worksheet.
3. Lightly merge the colors.

4. Fill the filbert brush with Warm White. Turn the bud upside down. Beginning at the tip, paint Warm White comma strokes into the wet undercoat colors. Continue, allowing the background color to show through until you reach the bottom. Study this carefully on the worksheet.
5. Using the #1 liner brush full of the thinned branch mixture (Raw Sienna and Burnt Umber), loosely and carefully outline the individual flowers on the bud.

The Wisteria Blossoms:

1. Apply blending gel medium to the clump of flowers.
2. Apply Prussian Blue, Pure Magenta, and Yellow Citron. Loosely blend the colors.
3. Using a #4 flat brush, create the four-petaled flowers in the wet colors you placed. This creates the shadowed flowers and provides the darkest value.
4. Wipe the brush. Quickly, while the background is wet, pick up Warm White. Paint four-petaled flowers, as shown on the worksheet, at random over the bunch. These are the middle or medium-value flowers.
5. Wipe the brush. Pick up Warm White and paint seven or nine light flowers randomly over the cluster. They are the lightest value flowers. It is important to

let the background flowers and darker values show through so that the wisteria is airy and loose. If the mass of flowers looks too solid, simply wipe the cluster from the outside edge in to remove them, and start again.

The Centers:

Paint the centers with a tiny dot of thinned Yellow Light and a tiny dot of Pure Black placed side by side. Don't let them be important or jump out at you.

The Curlicues:

Paint the curlicues using a #1 liner brush full of the thinned branch mixture (Raw Sienna and Burnt Umber). Use a very light touch and move the brush slowly. Be sure the handle of the brush points straight up towards the ceiling. Let dry and cure.

Finishing

1. Varnish with two or more coats waterbase varnish. Let dry.
2. Rub with a piece of brown paper bag with no printing on it to smooth the surface.
3. Apply a final coat of varnish or hand rub with paste wax. (This is hard work, but creates a beautiful finish.) □

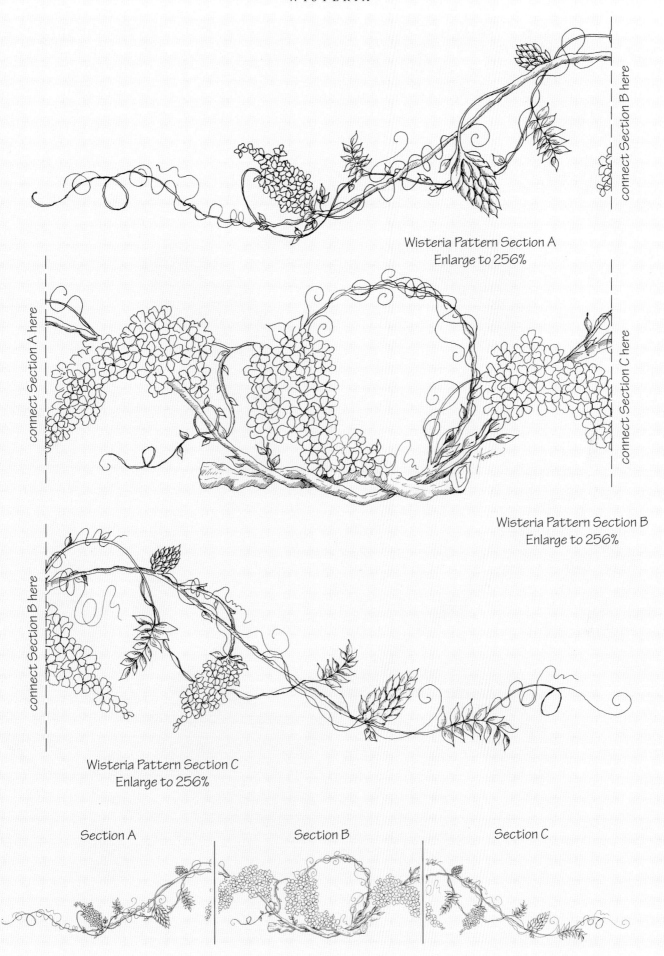

Wisteria Pattern Section A
Enlarge to 256%

connect Section B here

connect Section A here

connect Section C here

Wisteria Pattern Section B
Enlarge to 256%

connect Section B here

Wisteria Pattern Section C
Enlarge to 256%

Section A

Section B

Section C

Wisteria Worksheet

Step 1

Undercoat leaves with Green Medium.

Apply blending gel medium to bud and flower cluster. Apply colors. Lightly blend.

— Pure Magenta

— Prussian Blue

— Yellow Citron

Step 2

Shade leaves

Add strokes of Warm White to bud.

Stroke petals in the colors placed.

68

Wisteria Worksheet

Step 3

Pick up Warm White and stroke flower petals over the wet colors on the flower cluster.

Shade branch with floats of Burnt Umber.

Step 4

Outline strokes on bud with thinned Burnt Umber.

Add a few Warm White four-petaled flowers here and there. Add centers with dots of thinned Yellow Light and tiny dots of Pure Black.

June

June 6, 1985

Folk Art Tour I sponsored with Jacques and Michelle Zuidema

I'm in La Petite Pierre, a little castle village in the national park of the North Vosges. The national park is most inviting and particularly representative of the area. The woods of beach pine and oak trees bring renewed beauty to the landscapes in season. As I walk through the woods, at my feet are the most beautiful little for-get-me-nots. I'll have to sketch them now in a hurry in order to get back to the rest of the group. These woods are enchanting, I wish I had more time to spend here.

Forget-Me-Nots

Supplies

Artist's Acrylic Paints:
Burnt Umber
Green Dark
Green Light
Green Medium
Ice Blue
Olive Green Dark
Prussian Blue
Warm White
Yellow Light

Acrylic Craft Paints:
Bayberry
Licorice
Taffy

Mediums:
Blending gel medium
Glazing medium

Brushes:
Flats - #0, #4, #16
Liner - #1

Surface:
Twig-trimmed key keeper (this was unfinished wood)

Additional Supplies:
Old toothbrush
Gather the additional supplies that are listed in general "Supplies" section.

Preparation

1. Sand surface as needed to smooth. Wipe with a tack rag.
2. Basecoat with Taffy. Let dry.
3. Rub with a piece of brown paper bag with no printing on it to smooth the raised nap of the wood.
4. Neatly trace and transfer the design using gray graphite or colored chalk.

Painting

See the Forget-Me-Nots Worksheets on pages 76 and 77.

The Background Color:
The little tiny bit of background color can be added before or after the decorative painting is done.
1. Fill a #16 flat brush with glazing medium. Blot on a rag.
2. Place one corner of the brush in Olive Green Dark. Blend on the palette so that the color graduates through the hairs of the brush from dark to medium to light.
3. Pat the color on the upper section underneath the leaves, as shown on the worksheet. Let dry.

The Leaves:
1. Undercoat the leaves and the little flowers with two coats of Bayberry. Let dry.
2. Using a large brush, shade the base of the leaves with a float of Prussian Blue and glazing medium. Let dry.
3. Float again with Olive Green Dark.
4. Highlight the leaves with a float of Warm White and/or Ice Blue. Let dry.
5. To lighten a leaf here and there, wash with Green Light. Let dry.

The Forget-Me-Nots:
1. Undercoat the flowers with Bayberry plus Prussian Blue. Let dry.
2. Transfer the flower pattern.
3. Using a small, flat brush, pat on a tiny bit of blending gel medium to help the paint stay wet.
4. Pat on a tiny bit of Prussian Blue.
5. Fill a #0 flat brush with Warm White. Paint five comma strokes to create the little flower. (I paint a head, two arms, and two legs—this almost always creates a well-balanced flower.) Study this on the worksheet. Let some flowers be darker and some lighter. You can control this by occasionally wiping the brush and picking up more Warm White.

Instructions continued on page 74.

Instructions continued from page 72.

The Centers:

1. Apply a dot of very thin Yellow Light. Let dry.
2. Apply a tiny dot of very thin Licorice at the center of the yellow dot. Let dry.

The Linework & Curlicues:

Paint the linework and curlicues using the #1 liner brush and thinned Burnt Umber. Let dry and cure.

Finishing

1. Flyspeck, using an old toothbrush with thinned Burnt Umber. Practice first on a piece of copier paper, and then go to your project. Let dry.
2. Varnish with two or more coats of waterbase varnish. Let dry.
3. Rub with a piece of a brown paper bag with no printing on it to smooth the raised nap of the wood.
4. Apply a final coat of varnish. Let dry. ☐

Tips for Painting Linework

- Fill the brush good and full of thinned paint.
- Hold the brush so that the handle points straight up towards the ceiling.
- Paint slowly.

Forget-Me-Nots
Actual Size Pattern

Forget-Me-Nots Worksheet

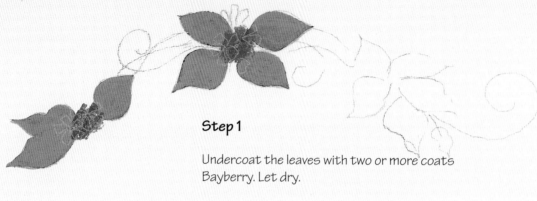

Step 1

Undercoat the leaves with two or more coats Bayberry. Let dry.

Undercoat the flowers with Bayberry plus Prussian Blue. Let dry. Transfer the flower pattern.

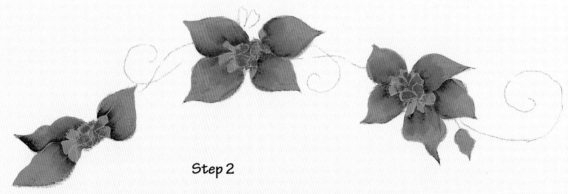

Step 2

Shade the leaves with floats of Prussian Blue.

Forget-Me-Nots Worksheet

Step 3

Apply a little blending gel medium to the flower petals.

Pat on a tiny bit of Prussian Blue.

Stroke the dark petals.

Stroke flower petals with Warm White.

Float leaves with Olive Green Dark. Let dry.

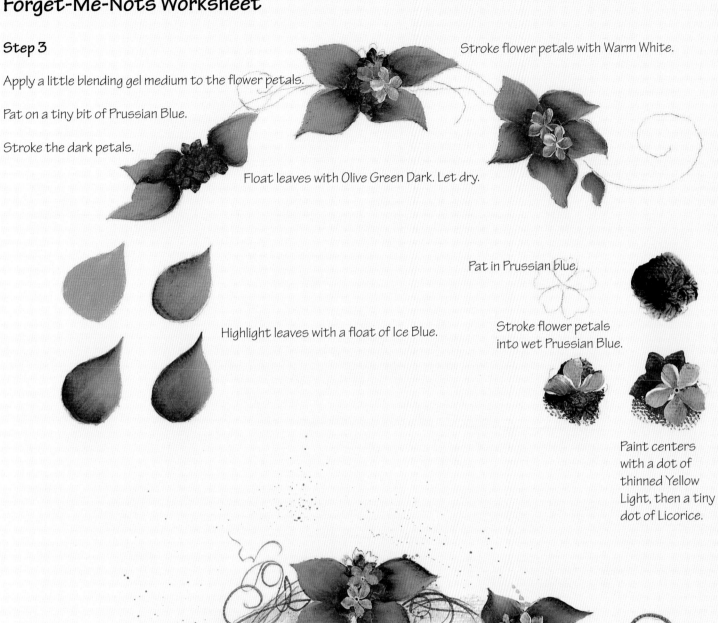

Highlight leaves with a float of Ice Blue.

Pat in Prussian blue.

Stroke flower petals into wet Prussian Blue.

Paint centers with a dot of thinned Yellow Light, then a tiny dot of Licorice.

Step 4

Paint curlicues with thinned Burnt Umber.

July

July 10, 1997

The years fly by so fast—
Leslie, is getting married and
I have so much to do. I want
to add all I can—by painting.
One thing is a family shower.
I've seen some adorable
watering cans with a baked-
on enamel finish at a craft
store. I'll buy them and
paint them with rosebuds,
leaves, and some little
white blossoms. I can fill
them with baby's breath and
real rosebuds and use them
as centerpieces. Then, if Leslie
wishes, she can use them for
bridesmaid's gifts.

Rosebuds & Blossoms

Supplies

Artist's Acrylic Paints:
Burnt Sienna
Green Dark
Ice Blue
Olive Green Dark
Prussian Blue
Red Light
Titanium White
True Burgundy
Yellow Light

Acrylic Craft Paint:
Bayberry

Mediums:
Floating medium
Glazing medium
Glass & Tile medium

Brushes:
Flats - #0, #2, #4, #6, #8, #10
Liner - #1

Surface:
Metal watering can (This one has a prefinished, high-gloss, baked-on enamel surface.)

Additional Supplies:
Gather the additional supplies that are listed in general "Supplies" section.

Rosebuds & Blossoms

Preparation

1. Wash the watering can thoroughly with soap and water. Let dry completely.
2. Transfer the design, using gray graphite paper.
3. To create a better painting surface on the slick watering can, apply glass and tile medium to the design area only. Be sure you get a good, even coverage. Let dry and cure for one week.

Painting

See the Rosebuds & Blossoms Worksheets on pages 84 and 85.

Because of this metal surface, floating medium is used to undercoat the design areas so that the paint will move and float easier on the surface.

The Leaves:

1. Undercoat the leaves with two coats of Bayberry. Let the paint dry thoroughly between each coat. Let cure thoroughly.
2. Apply floating medium to the painted leaves. With floating medium still on brush, dip corner of brush into Green Dark to prepare for floating. While floating medium is still wet on leaf, float the shadows on the leaves with Green Dark.
3. Highlight the leaves with a float of Ice Blue.

The Stems:

1. Using a liner brush and thinned Bayberry, paint the stems. Let dry.
2. Shade with Green Dark.

The Rosebuds:

1. Undercoat the rosebuds with True Burgundy. Let dry and cure.

2. Apply a little glazing medium to rosebuds. Apply a dark center, using a dark mixture of equal amounts of True Burgundy and Red Light (1:1).
3. Double-load a #4 flat brush with the dark mixture and a mixture of Titanium White and the dark mixture (2:1). Blend on the palette to soften the color.
4. Paint an upside-down u-stroke to create the upper portion of the bud. (You may go over this again, if needed.)
5. Paint a u-stroke to create the lower portion of the bud. Study this on the worksheet. Let dry.
6. Using a liner brush, add dots of thinned Titanium White in the centers, as shown on the worksheet. Let dry.

The Blossoms:

1. Neatly transfer the blossom design on the painted leaves and rosebuds.
2. Carefully undercoat the blossoms using #0 flat brush with Titanium White. A second coat and possibly a third coat may be needed to cover. Let dry and cure.
3. Using the #0 flat brush, shade each petal where it joins the center with a float of Olive Green Dark.

4. Carefully paint the centers with Yellow Light. Let dry.
5. Shade the centers with a float of Burnt Sienna. Let dry.
6. Add tiny dots of Titanium White around the center. Study this on the worksheet.
7. Add a few filler dots with a mix of Prussian Blue and Titanium White (1:4).

The Ribbon:

1. Using a liner brush full of thinned Prussian Blue, paint fine lines to create the string bow and streamers.
2. Highlight the ribbon using the liner brush and thinned Ice Blue.

The Curlicues:

Paint the curlicues using the liner brush with thinned Olive Green Dark. It will be necessary to go back over them a second or third time since the background is so slick. Let dry and cure.

Finishing

Apply a coat of glass and tile medium or waterbase varnish over the painted design only. Let dry. ☐

Tips for Painting on Glossy Surfaces

These statements are true for almost everything you paint, but are particularly applicable for the slick, baked-on enamel finish of the watering can.

- Let every one of the undercoats dry and cure thoroughly.
- Curing can take as long as a week, depending upon the humidity and the temperature of the area in which are you working. If the paint has not cured long enough, the undercoat could lift when a float is applied.

Rosebuds & Blossoms
Actual Size Pattern

Rosebuds & Blossoms Worksheet

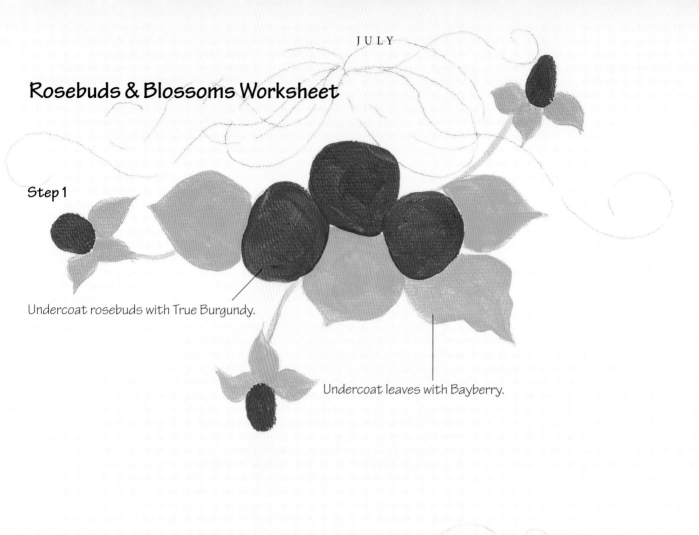

Step 1

Undercoat rosebuds with True Burgundy.

Undercoat leaves with Bayberry.

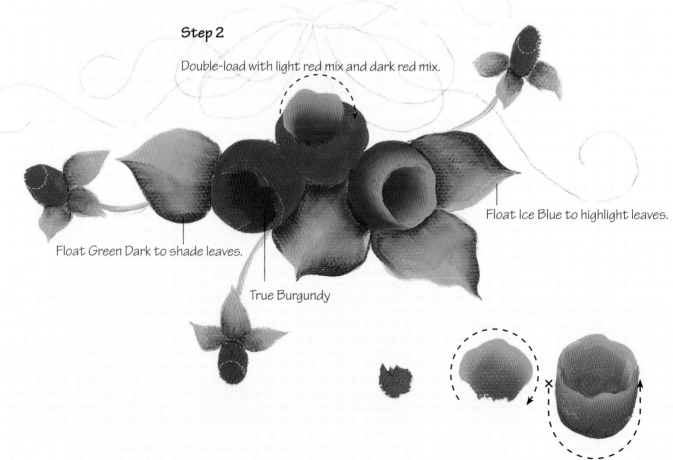

Step 2

Double-load with light red mix and dark red mix.

Float Green Dark to shade leaves.

True Burgundy

Float Ice Blue to highlight leaves.

Rosebuds & Blossoms Worksheet

Step 3

Paint bow with mixes of Prussian
Blue and Titanium White.

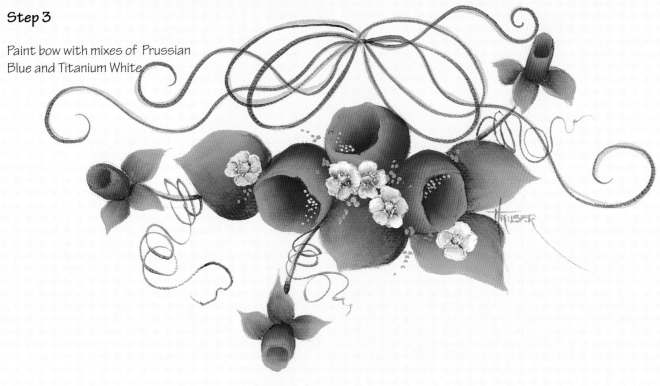

Small Blossoms

Paint blossoms with Titanium White.

Paint center with Yellow Light.

Petals - Shade with a float of Olive Green
Dark.

Center - Shade with Burnt Sienna.

Add dots of Olive Green Dark and Titanium
White.

August

August 21, 1989

I just returned from Miss JoAnn's patio tea party. The tables were beautifully set and the centerpieces were unique, but I couldn't take my eyes off of the flower boxes that lined the patio. They were full of zinnias blooming in the strong, bold colors of summer. Few flowers have such vibrant color. I studied these flowers for quite sometime, and then I simply had to sketch them. Because of their many petals - it will take a little more time to paint them.

Zinnias

Supplies

Artist's Acrylic Paints:
Burnt Sienna
Burnt Umber
Green Dark
Green Light
Green Medium
Olive Green Dark
Pure Orange
Raw Sienna
Red Light
True Burgundy
Warm White
Yellow Light

Acrylic Craft Paint:
Lipstick Red

Medium:
Glazing medium

Brushes:
Flats - #2, #4, #6, #8, #10
Liner - #1

Surface:
Basket with hinged wooden top (This basket was already stained and the lid was waxed, not varnished.)

Additional Supplies:
Gather the additional supplies that are listed in general "Supplies" section.

Preparation

1. Sand the lid with a fine grade of sandpaper to remove the wax. Wipe with a tack rag. *See sidebar for instructions for preparing an unfinished basket on page 90.*
2. Transfer the design using White graphite paper.

Painting

See the Zinnias Worksheet on page 91.

The Leaves:
1. Undercoat the leaves with two coats of Green Medium. Let dry and cure.
2. Using glazing medium and Green Dark, float shadows at the base of each leaf. Let dry.
3. Float a second shadow with Olive Green Dark. Let dry.
4. Float Warm White on the light or right edges of the leaves. Let dry.
5. Apply a wash of Green Light on the leaf to brighten the color. Let dry.

The Stems:
1. Paint the stems with Green Medium.
2. Shade with Green Dark and Olive Green Dark.

The Yellow Zinnia:
1. Carefully undercoat the entire flower shape with Raw Sienna. Let dry. Apply a second coat, if needed to cover. Let dry.
2. Using White graphite paper or chalk, transfer all of the petals to the flower.
3. Beginning with the outside row of petals, shade the outside edge of each petal by floating on Yellow Light. Let dry. If needed, apply a second coat to lighten.
4. Float the shadow at the base of each petal with Burnt Sienna.
5. Highlight a petal here and there with Warm White.

The Red Zinnia:
1. Undercoat the entire flower shape with Lipstick Red. Let dry. If needed, apply a second coat to cover. Let dry.
2. Using White graphite paper or chalk, transfer all of the petals to the flower.
3. Beginning with the outside row of petals, shade the outside edge of each petal by floating on Red Light. Let dry. If needed, apply a second coat to lighten.
4. Float the shadow at the base of each petal with True Burgundy. If needed, apply a second coat to darken. Let dry.
5. Highlight an occasional petal with Pure Orange.

The Centers:
1. Paint the centers with Burnt Umber. A second or even a third coat will be needed to cover. Let dry.
2. Using a liner brush and thinned Yellow Light, paint tiny dots in the shape of an oval around the upper half of the center. Study the worksheet.
3. Add a few dots of Yellow Light and a few dots of Warm White around the bottom of the center.

Instructions continued on page 90

Instructions continued from page 88

The Curlicues:
Paint the curlicues using the liner brush and thinned Burnt Umber. Let dry and cure.

Finishing

1. Apply two or more coats waterbase varnish. Let dry.
2. Rub with a piece of brown paper bag with no printing on it to smooth the raised surface.
3. Apply a final coat of varnish. Let dry. ☐

To Prepare an Unfinished Basket

1. Sand the lid. Wipe with a tack rag.
2. Mix a stain of two parts glazing medium and one part paint in the color of your choice.
3. Apply the stain with a sponge brush or a slightly dampened cotton rag. Let dry. If a deeper stain is desired, stain a second time. Let dry.
4. Transfer the pattern.

Here's a Tip:
When staining a woven basket, I use a small piece of kitchen sponge so that I can squeeze the stain into the weave of the basket. Then I wipe inside and outside to remove the excess stain.

Zinnias
Actual Size Pattern

Zinnias Worksheet

Step 1
Undercoat petals with Lipstick Red.

Undercoat leaves with Green Medium.

Shade with Green Dark.

Step 2

Shade dark petals with True Burgundy.

Shade light petals with Red Light.

Step 3

Highlight petals with Pure Orange.

Paint center with Burnt Umber.

Deepen shading with Olive Green Dark.

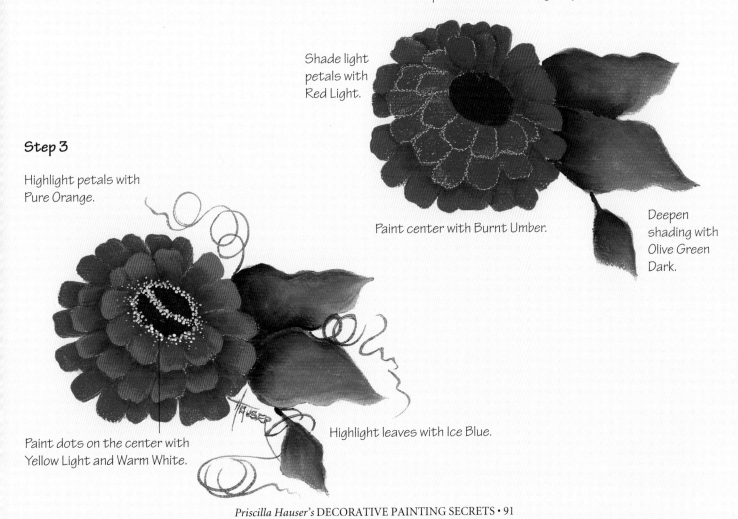

Highlight leaves with Ice Blue.

Paint dots on the center with Yellow Light and Warm White.

September

September 12, 1970

The wild roses are still in full bloom. There are so many different varieties and beautiful colors. They climb the brick wall at the back of my garden. I imagine they'll keep blooming until winter arrives. They move so gracefully in the late summer breeze, that as I sketch them, I can twist and turn them to fit a variety of different surfaces.

Wild Roses

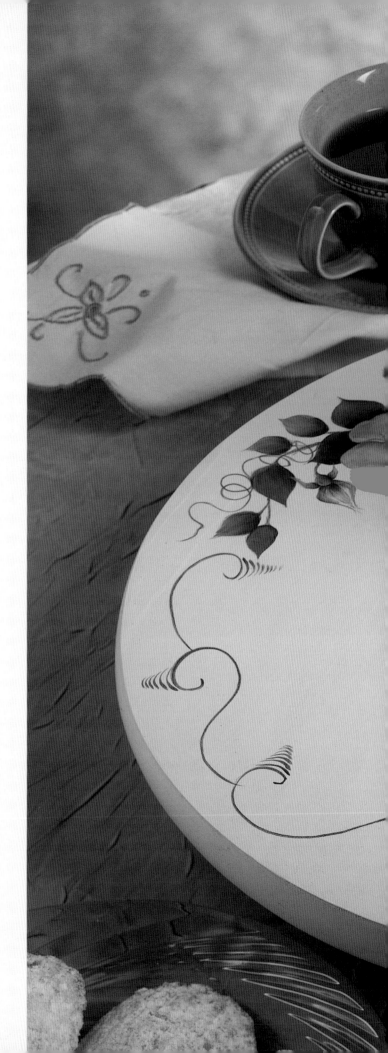

Supplies

Artist's Acrylic Paints:
Burnt Sienna
Burnt Umber
Green Dark
Green Light
Green Medium
Payne's Gray
Raw Sienna
Red Light
Titanium White
Yellow Citron
Yellow Light

Acrylic Craft Paint:
Taffy

Mediums:
Floating medium
Blending gel medium
Glazing medium

Brushes:
Flats - #2, #4, #6, #8, #10
Liner - #1

Surface:
Wooden lazy susan, unfinished wood

Additional Supplies:
Gather the additional supplies that are listed in general "Supplies" section.

Preparation

1. Sand the lazy susan, if needed. Wipe with a tack rag.
2. Basecoat with two coats of Taffy, letting the paint dry between each coat.
3. When dry, rub with a piece of brown paper bag with no printing on it to smooth the nap of the wood.
4. Neatly trace and transfer the design, using colored chalk.

Painting

See the Wild Roses Worksheets on pages 98 and 99.

Leaves:

1. Undercoat the leaves with two coats of Green Medium. Let dry.
2. Using as large a flat brush as you comfortably can, float (with glazing medium) Green Dark at the base of each leaf.
3. Float Burnt Sienna here and there to give some color variation to the leaves.
4. To softly highlight, float on a little Ice Blue at random.

The Stems:

1. Fill the liner brush good and full with very thin Green Light. Paint the stems.
2. Shade with Burnt Umber.
3. Highlight with a little Raw Sienna.

The Wild Roses:

1. Paint the petals with Titanium White. Let dry.
2. Make a light red mixture of Titanium White and Red Light (2:1).
3. Lightly dampen the petals with a little floating medium or glazing medium.
4. Float the light red mixture around the outside edge of the petals, using as large a flat brush as you comfortably can. (I used a #10.) Let dry. Apply a second or even a third coat, as desired, to deepen the coral color of the petals. Let dry.
5. To further deepen the petal color, make a mixture of Red Light and Burnt Sienna (1:1).
6. Float the darker shadows under the turned edges of the petals and in the shadowed areas of the petals. Let dry.
7. Using as large a flat brush as possible, float a tiny touch of Payne's Gray at the center of each petal. Let dry.
8. Float on a tiny touch of Yellow Citron.

The Centers:

1. Using a small flat brush, paint the centers with Yellow Light. Let dry.
2. Shade with a float of Burnt Sienna. Let dry.
3. To create the indentation in the center, use a very small flat brush and float a sideways u-stroke of Burnt Sienna. Study this on the worksheet.

4. Using a #1 liner brush filled with very thin Payne's Gray, paint fine lines coming from the center and flowing gracefully onto each petal.
5. Add lines with Payne's Gray and dots with Burnt Sienna, Yellow Light, and Titanium White. Study the worksheet for details.

The Buds:

1. Paint the buds with the light red mixture. Let dry. Apply a second coat, if needed.
2. Paint the bracts with Green Light.
3. Shade with Green Dark.
4. Highlight with Titanium White.

The Curlicues & Details:

1. Paint using a liner brush full of thinned Burnt Umber.
2. Paint over them a second a time with Raw Sienna. Let dry and cure.

Finishing

1. Apply two or more coats waterbase varnish. Let dry.
2. Rub with a piece of brown paper bag with no printing on it to smooth the raised surface.
3. Apply a final coat of varnish or rub with paste wax. ☐

Wild Roses
Enlarge to 167%

Wild Roses Worksheet

Step 1

Undercoat leaves with Green Medium. Let dry.

Paint center with Yellow Light.

Step 2

Float Green Dark at the base of each leaf. Let dry.

Float Burnt Sienna on the leaves here and there.

Step 3

Add a "C" float of Burnt Sienna in the center.

Paint fine lines with Payne's Gray. Add dots with Burnt Sienna, Yellow Light, and Titanium White.

Wild Roses Worksheet

Step 4
Paint the petals with Titanium White.

Step 5
Float the red mixture on the petals. Let dry.

Step 6
Float the darker red mix on the petals. Float on a touch of Payne's Gray.

Let dry. Float on a touch of Yellow Citron.

October

October 2, 1989

Today, driving from the airport across the Delaware countryside, the road was lined with Queen Anne's Lace. I'd never seen them so large. I asked my driver to stop so I could pick some to sketch. I think it would be difficult to paint each individual flower - they are so light and airy - so delicate. I'll use a sponge to paint them or --- make one of those wonderful rubberband brushes!

Queen Anne's Lace

Supplies

Artist's Acrylic Paints:
Green Dark
Green Light
Green Medium
Olive Green Dark
Warm White
Yellow Citron

Acrylic Craft Paint:
Clover

Mediums:
Floating medium
Blending gel medium

Brushes:
Flats - #4
Liner - #1
An old, beat-up ("scruffy") flat brush or a
rubber-band brush (See page 104 for how to
make one.)

Surface:
Willow basket with hinged rusty tin lid

Additional Supplies:
Rubber bands, 25 - 50
Gather the additional supplies that are
listed in general "Supplies" section.

Preparation

1. Wipe the rusty tin lid with a damp rag. Let dry.
2. Using white chalk or white graphite paper, transfer the traced design. (It's **not** necessary to try to transfer the little flowers, only a general outline. It **is** important to transfer all the little stems that go up into the cluster of flowers.)

Painting

See the Queen Anne's Lace Worksheet.

The Leaves & Stems:

1. Undercoat the leaves with Clover. Two or three coats will be needed to achieve a smooth, even coverage. Let dry and cure.
2. Undercoat the stems in Clover. Let dry and cure.
3. Shade the leaves with a float (using floating medium) of Green Dark. Let dry. Deepen with a float of Olive Green Dark. Let dry.
4. Highlight the leaves with a float of Warm White. Let dry.
5. Shade the stems, using the liner brush with thinned Green Dark.

6. Deepen the shading with Olive Green Dark. Let dry.
7. Highlight the stems with thinned Warm White. Let dry.

Queen Anne's Lace:

1. Dab on the flowers using a scruffy brush or rubber band brush, using very little thinned Warm White. To do this, first dip the brush in the thinned paint. Blot on a rag. Lightly and loosely dab the color on the flower. Practice this technique several times before applying it to your surface. Let dry.
   • Keep the flowers very light and airy.
   • Always blot off excess paint from brush before applying it to the surface.
2. If desired, use the liner brush with thinned paint to add a few four-petal flowers here and there. Let dry.
3. Wash on a tiny bit of Yellow Citron to create a little yellow-green shading.

The Curlicues:

1. Paint the curlicues with the #1 liner brush and thinned Green Light.
2. Go over them a second time with Green Medium. Let dry and cure.

Finishing

1. Apply two or more coats of waterbase varnish. Let dry.
2. Rub with a piece of brown paper bag with no printing on it to smooth the raised surface.
3. Apply a final coat of varnish or rub with clear paste wax. □

How to Make a Rubber Band Brush

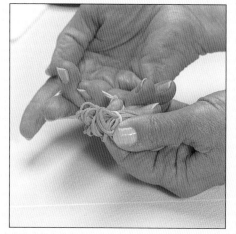

Photo 1. Gather 25 to 50 rubber bands. Fold in half. Tightly wrap another rubber band around them, at one end.

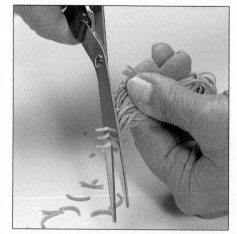

Photo 2. Cut off looped ends.

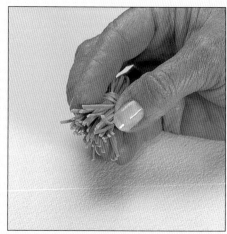

Photo 3. This now makes a great brush for dabbing.

Queen Anne's Lace Worksheet

Undercoat leaves with Clover.

Shade with floats of Green Dark.

Dab flowers with thinned Warm White.

Wash a tiny touch of Yellow Citron on

the flowers. Highlight leaves and stems with

Warm White.

Paint a few tiny four-petal blossoms on the large flower

Queen Ann's Lace
Actual Size Pattern

Chrysanthemums

Enlarge to 134%

See Project Instructions
on Page 110

November

November 20, 1998

In 1932, mother was crowned the first Engineering Queen on the University of Tulsa campus. Needless to say, I wasn't there to see it happen, but in later years, the past queens would often be honored at Homecoming games. Mother was always presented with a huge football chrysanthemum.

Beautiful, long streaming ribbons would flow from this large flower. There are so many different types of chrysanthemums in an array of wonderful colors.

Because their many petals are shaped like comma strokes, they are fast to draw and even faster to paint.

Chrysanthemums

Supplies

Artist's Acrylic Paints:
Burnt Sienna
Green Light
Green Medium
Medium Yellow
Olive Green Dark
Red Light
Warm White
Yellow Citron

Acrylic Craft Paint:
Clover

Mediums:
Floating medium
Blending gel medium
Glazing medium

Brushes:
Flats - #8, #10
Liner - #1
Filbert - #6

Surface:
Frosted glass platter

Additional Supplies:
Gather the additional supplies that are listed in general "Supplies" section.

Preparation

See pattern on page 107.
Neatly trace and transfer the pattern, using gray graphite paper.

Painting

See the Chrysanthemum Worksheets on pages 112 and 113.

The Leaves:
You may vary the amount of light and dark colors you use in the leaf. This will create interest and variation. Often leaves that are to the back of a design or underneath are the darkest. The lighter leaves can be found closer to the top of the design.

1. Undercoat the leaves with two or more coats of Clover. Let dry and cure.
2. Double-load a large flat brush with floating medium and Olive Green Dark. Blend on the palette to graduate the colors from dark to medium to clear.
3. Float Olive Green Dark on the base of each leaf and along the dark side. Study this on the color worksheet. Let dry.
4. Float a little Burnt Sienna at the base of each leaf. Let dry.
5. Apply a small amount of glazing medium to the leaf. Add Olive Green Dark at the base, Green Light in the middle, and Warm White on the light side. Wipe the brush and lightly blend, pulling from the base of the leaf out to the edges and lightly blending back from the outer edges towards the base. Study this on the worksheet. Let dry.

6. If desired, wash a little Burnt Sienna or Green Light on the leaf for additional color.

The Chrysanthemum:
1. Undercoat the chrysanthemums with two or more coats of Burnt Sienna. Let dry and cure.
2. Apply blending gel medium, then apply the flower colors (Yellow Citron, Medium Yellow, and Burnt Sienna). Lightly blend.
3. Fill the filbert brush with Warm White that has  been thinned with water to the consistency of flowing cream. Paint two comma strokes opposite each other at the top of the flower, as shown on the worksheet. Continue painting the comma strokes, pulling to the base of the ball shape or the X. *(see photo)* Do not pick up more Warm White unless you have to—you want to catch the wet color and let it flow back into the stroke you are making.
4. Turn the flower upside down. If necessary, add a little bit more blending gel medium and Burnt Sienna. Paint the lower petals of the flower, working in towards the X at the base of the ball. A second row of strokes may be added here or there, if needed.

The Curlicues:
1. Fill the #1 liner brush with thinned Olive Green Dark. Hold the handle of the liner brush so that it points straight up towards the ceiling and paint slowly.
2. Go back over the curlicues with a little Burnt Umber. (When I do this, I don't try to match the first lines.) Let dry and cure.

Finishing

Apply two or more coats of waterbase varnish to the design area only. Let dry.
To clean: Wipe the plate with a damp rag and dry it. Do not put it in the dishwasher. □

Tips for Painting Chrysanthemums

- Study the pattern. I have divided the chrysanthemum in two sections. The upper portion is a ball with an X at the bottom. The lower portion is comma strokes that draw to the X. Paint the upper portion or ball first, then turn the flower upside down and paint the lower portion, pulling the comma strokes in towards the X at the base of the ball.
- It is important to let this flower breathe. Let some of the background color show through. Don't paint it as a solid mass of strokes.
- If you don't like what you paint, use a damp rag and wipe from the outside edge in towards the center to remove the strokes. Put the blending gel and the colors back down and start again.

Chrysanthemum Worksheet

Step 1
Undercoat the flower with Burnt Sienna.

Step 2
Undercoat the leaves with Clover.

Apply blending gel medium.

Yellow Citron

Medium Yellow

Burnt Sienna

Blend

Step 3
Paint comma strokes on wet paint with Warm White.

Add more blending gel medium and Burnt Sienna.

Float on Olive Green Dark.

Step 4
Float Burnt Sienna at base of leaf.

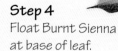

Finish the flower petal strokes.

Chrysanthemum Worksheet

Step 5
Apply glazing medium to the leaf.

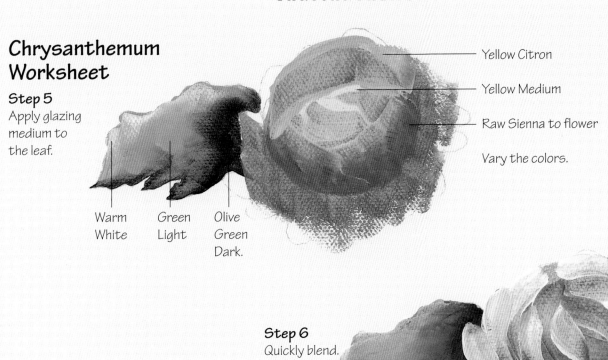

Warm White

Green Light

Olive Green Dark.

Yellow Citron

Yellow Medium

Raw Sienna to flower

Vary the colors.

Step 6
Quickly blend.

Step 7
Wash more colors on leaves, if needed.

Finished flower

December

December 1, 1995

I've learned that time is the most precious gift I can give. Time spent creating hand-painted gifts is time well spent and a hand-painted glass ornament seems to be so appreciated by everyone I've ever given one to. I'm going to draw my Flowers of the Month to paint and give this holiday season.

Crocus

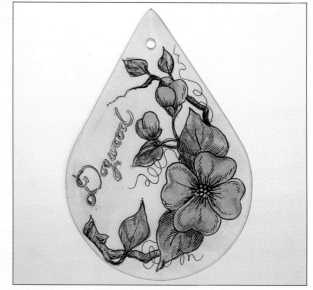

Dogwood

Lily of the Valley

Blossoms

Wisteria

Forget-Me-Nots

Rosebud

Zinnia

Wild Rose

Queen Anne's Lace

Chrysanthemum

Holly & Berries

December

Supplies

Artist's Acrylic Paints:
Alizarin Crimson
Burnt Umber
Dioxazine Purple
Green Dark
Green Light
Green Medium
Green Umber
Ice Blue Light
Light Red Oxide
Medium Yellow
Naphthol Crimson
Payne's Gray
Prussian Blue
Titanium White
Turner's Yellow

Mediums:
Floating medium
Blending gel medium

Brushes:
Flats - #0, #2
Liner - #1

Surfaces:
12 etched glass ornaments

Additional Supplies:
Technical inking pens - #00, #1
Technical pen ink - Black
Gold marking pen
Clear matte acrylic spray sealer
Double-sided cellophane tape
Gather the additional supplies that are listed in general "Supplies" section.

Preparation
1. Lightly mist the ornaments with matte acrylic spray varnish. Let dry.
2. Trace the pattern. Reduce or enlarge to the size of the ornament. Apply a piece of double-sided tape to the front of the traced pattern. Place the ornament over the traced design.

Painting
Create very thin, transparent washes with water and just a touch of color. Apply the color and let dry thoroughly. Then ink using the technical pen and technical pen ink. See the Flower Ornament Worksheet.

Crocus:
1. Leaves - Make various mixtures of Green Medium and Medium Yellow. Wash the mixes on the leaves. Shade with Green Dark.
2. Flower - Mix Titanium White and Dioxazine Purple (2:1) and wash this color on the flower. Shade with Dioxazine Purple.
3. Snow - Wash on Titanium White. Shade with Payne's Gray.

Dogwood:
1. Leaves - Wash on Green Medium. Shade with Green Dark. Highlight with Medium Yellow.
2. Petals - Wash with Titanium White. Tip the edges with a wash of Naphthol Crimson plus Titanium White.
3. Center - Wash on Green Medium.
4. Stem - Wash on Burnt Umber.

Lily of the Valley:
1. Leaves - Wash with Green Medium. Shade with Green Dark.
2. Blooms - Wash on Titanium White.
3. Buds - Wash on Titanium White plus a touch of Green Umber.
4. Stem - Wash with Medium Yellow plus Titanium White.
5. Trim - Wash with Titanium White. Shade with gold ink.

Blossoms:
1. Leaves - Wash with Green Medium. Shade with Olive Green Dark.
2. Blossoms - Wash with Titanium White. Shade with Payne's Gray plus Titanium White plus a touch of Olive Green Dark.
3. Buds - Wash with Titanium White. Shade with the same mixture used on the blossoms.

Wisteria:
1. Leaves - Wash on Green Medium. Shade with Olive Green Dark.
2. Stem - Wash with Burnt Umber. Shade with Burnt Umber.
3. Blooms - Wash with Titanium White plus a little Prussian Blue. To vary the bloom colors, wash with the Prussian Blue mixture plus Alizarin Crimson.

Forget-Me-Nots:
1. Leaves - Wash with Green Medium. Shade with Green Dark.
2. Stems - Wash with Burnt Umber. Highlight with Turner's Yellow.
3. Flowers - Wash with various mixtures of Titanium White and Prussian Blue.
4. Flower Centers - Wash with Turner's Yellow.

The Rosebud:
1. Leaves - Apply a thin wash of Green Light. Let dry. Shade, if desired, with Green Dark.
2. Buds - Mix Titanium White plus a touch of Alizarin Crimson to make a pink. Wash this color on the buds. Shade the centers with Alizarin Crimson.
3. Bow - Mix Titanium White plus a tiny

touch of Prussian Blue. Wash this color on the bow.

The Zinnia:
1. Leaves - Wash on Green Medium. Shade with Green Dark.
2. Flower - Wash the petals with Medium Yellow. Shade with Light Red Oxide.
3. Flower Center - Wash with Medium Yellow. Shade with Light Red Oxide. Highlight with Titanium White. Paint dots with thinned Medium Yellow and Titanium White.

The Wild Rose:
1. Leaves - Wash on Green Medium. Shade with Green Dark.
2. Petals - Mix Titanium White and Naphthol Crimson (1:1). Wash this color on the petals. Shade with Naphthol Crimson.
3. Center - Mix Medium Yellow and Titanium White (1:1). Wash this color on the center. Shade with Light Red Oxide.

Queen Anne's Lace:
1. Leaves - Wash on Green Medium. Shade with Green Dark. Highlight with Medium Yellow.

2. Flowers - Wash with Titanium White.
3. Stem - Wash with Green Medium. Shade with Green Dark.

The Chrysanthemum:
1. Leaves - Wash on Green Medium. Shade with Green Dark. Highlight with Medium Yellow.
2. Flower Petals - Wash with Medium Yellow at the top. Shade with Light Red Oxide at the bottom.

Holly & Berries:
1. Ribbon - Wash with Titanium White. Shade with Payne's Gray.
2. Leaves - Wash on a mixture of Green Dark plus a touch of Prussian Blue. Highlight with Ice Blue.
3. Berries - Wash on Naphthol Crimson. Shade with a tiny touch of Payne's Gray. Highlight with Ice Blue.

Finishing

1. Do the lettering with the gold pen. Let dry five hours before varnishing.
2. Outline with black ink as shown. Let dry and cure.
3. Lightly mist with clear acrylic sealer spray. ☐

Flower Ornament Worksheet

Blossoms:
Wash

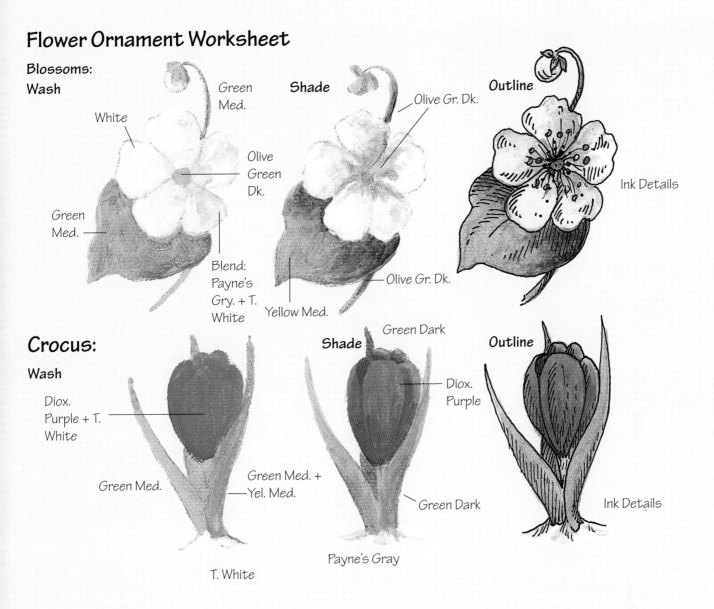

White

Green Med.

Shade

Olive Gr. Dk.

Olive Green Dk.

Outline

Green Med.

Ink Details

Blend: Payne's Gry. + T. White

Olive Gr. Dk.

Yellow Med.

Crocus:

Wash

Diox. Purple + T. White

Green Med.

Green Med. + Yel. Med.

Shade

Green Dark

Diox. Purple

Green Dark

Outline

Ink Details

T. White

Payne's Gray

Forget-Me-Nots:

Wash

Prussian Blue + T. White

Green Med.

Shade

Yellow Med.

Outline

Ink Details

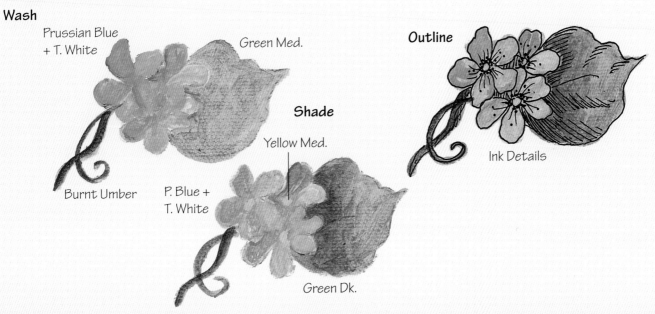

Burnt Umber

P. Blue + T. White

Green Dk.

Flower Ornament Worksheet

Dogwood:

Wash

T. White

Green Med.

Burnt Umber

Green. Med.

Blend

Napthol Crimson + T. white

Outline

Green Med.

Green Dk.

Yellow Med.

Outline

Ink details

Queen Anne's Lace:

Wash

T. White

Green Med.

Blend

Outline

Green Dk.

Yellow Med.

Green Dk.

Outline

Ink details

Zinnia:

Wash

Yellow Med.

Burnt Umber

Green Med.

Blend

Green Dk.

Lt. Red. Oxide

Burnt Umber

Outline

Outline

Ink details

Flower Ornament Worksheet

Lily of the Valley:

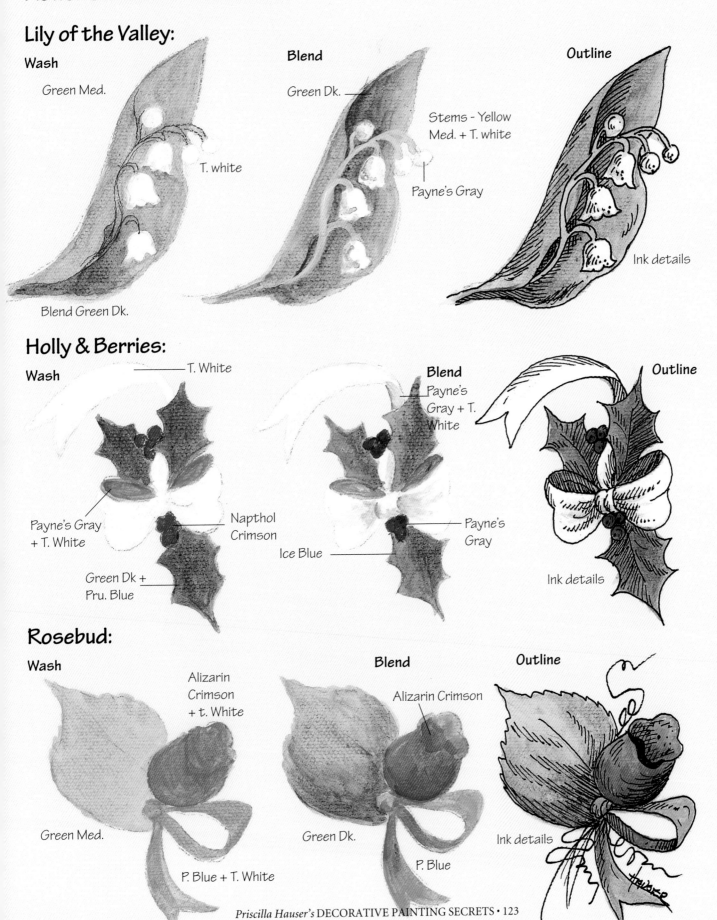

Wash

Green Med.

T. white

Blend Green Dk.

Blend

Green Dk.

Stems - Yellow Med. + T. white

Payne's Gray

Outline

Ink details

Holly & Berries:

Wash

T. White

Payne's Gray + T. White

Napthol Crimson

Green Dk + Pru. Blue

Blend

Payne's Gray + T. White

Ice Blue

Payne's Gray

Outline

Ink details

Rosebud:

Wash

Alizarin Crimson + t. White

Green Med.

P. Blue + T. White

Blend

Alizarin Crimson

Green Dk.

P. Blue

Outline

Ink details

Flower Ornament Worksheet

Wild Rose:

Wash

Yellow Med.

Napthol
Crimson +
T. White

Green Med.

Shade

Napthol
Crimson

Lt. Red
Oxide

T. White

Green Dk.

Outline

Ink details

Wisteria:

Wash
Burnt Umber

Pr. Blue +
T. White

Green
Med.

Shade

Burnt
Umber

Olive Green Dk.

P. Blue +
Aliz. Crimson +
T. White

T. White
+ P. Blue

Outline

Ink details

Chrysanthemum:

Wash

Yellow Med.

Green Med.

Blend

Yel. Med. + Lt. Red Oxide

Green Dk.
Yellow Med.

Outline
Ink details

Dogwood

Queen Anne's Lace

Zinnia

Actual Size Patterns

See pages 126 and 127 for
additional patterns.

Holly and Berries

Lilly of the Valley

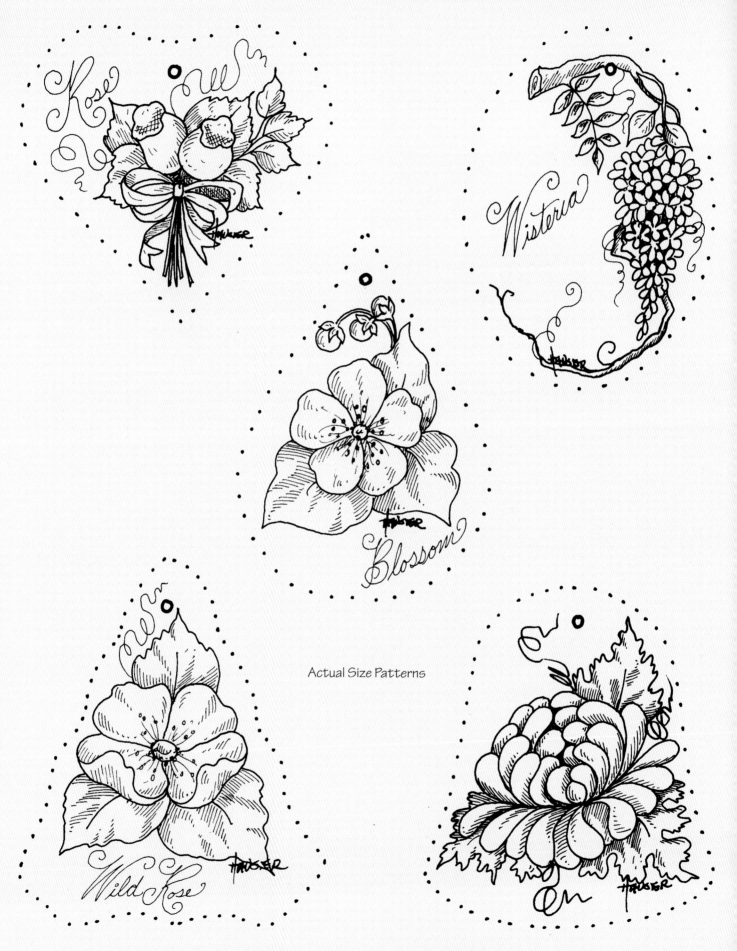

Actual Size Patterns

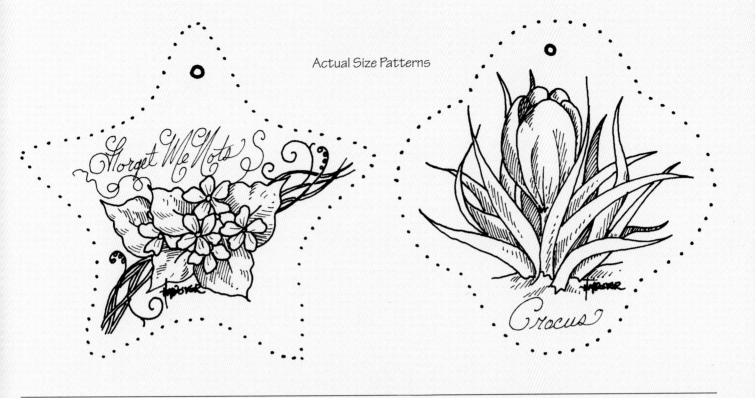

Actual Size Patterns

Metric Conversion Chart

Inches to Millimeters and Centimeters

Inches	MM	CM	Inches	MM	CM	Inches	MM	CM
1/8	3	.3	1	25	2.5	6	152	15.2
1/4	6	.6	1-1/4	32	3.2	7	178	17.8
3/8	10	1.0	1-1/2	38	3.8	8	203	20.3
1/2	13	1.3	1-3/4	44	4.4	9	229	22.9
5/8	16	1.6	2	51	5.1	10	254	25.4
3/4	19	1.9	3	76	7.6	11	279	27.9
7/8	22	2.2	4	102	10.2	12	305	30.5
			5	127	12.7			

Yards to Meters

Yards	Meters	Yards	Meters
1/8	.11	3	2.74
1/4	.23	4	3.66
3/8	.34	5	4.57
1/2	.46	6	5.49
5/8	.57	7	6.40
3/4	.69	8	7.32
7/8	.80	9	8.23
1	.91	10	9.14
2	1.83		

Index